DATE		
AUG 1 '91		
AUG 4 '91		
NOV 5 '92		
DEC 14 '92		
MAY 3 1993		
SEP 21 2022		

Roots of a Black Future: Family and Church

Books by J. Deotis Roberts
Published by The Westminster Press

Roots of a Black Future: Family and Church

A Black Political Theology

Liberation and Reconciliation: A Black Theology

Roots of a Black Future: Family and Church

J. Deotis Roberts

The Westminster Press
Philadelphia

First edition

Published by The Westminster Press ®

Philadelphia, Pennsylvania

PRINTED IN THE UNITED STATES OF AMERICA
9 8 7 6 5 4 3 2 1

Library of Congress Cataloging in Publication Data

Roberts, James Deotis.
  Roots of a Black future.

  Includes bibliographical references.
    1. Afro-Americans—Religion. 2. Afro-American families. 3. Black theology. I. Title.
BR563.N4R62   261.8'358   80–16788
ISBN 0–664–24333–9

Contents

Preface

Two primary institutions have nurtured blacks in the United States. These are the church and the family. It has been my intention for several years to write a theological treatise relating these two institutions. Other duties have made delay unavoidable. But the urgency of the task has prevailed upon me. The present work is the result of this deeply felt concern.

Because the author is a theologian, all his instincts are guided by that fact. The discussion will move freely in several disciplines, but disciplines other than theology will serve the ends of theological reflection. We will be interested in the family as a symbol of a deeper understanding of the church. At the same time, considerable attention will be given to the role of family and church as "visible" institutions and to their humanizing functions in the lives of black people.

The church will be considered both as an organ of the spirit and as an organization. We will look at the history of the whole church of God and view the black church in the context of this stream of development. The African roots of the black church will be explored. The black church as "invisible" and "visible" will be discussed. We will, therefore, desire to examine the nature and the mission of the black church, giving due consideration to its distinctive heritage and its liberating and healing ministry.

The black family will be understood in an "extended" rather than a "nuclear" sense. The family will express for us the meaning of community. This concept of communalism will be traced through the African/Afro-American heritage of social and religious experience. We will draw out the pedagogical, psychological, and social significance of the family for the sanity, health, and wholeness of black people.

Then there will be an attempt to use theological discourse to express the deep significance of family and church in the experience and survival of black people. The Biblical background will have a large place in our discussion, as will the history of doctrine. But there will be a conscious affinity with the theologies of liberation and all Third World theological developments.

While the main purpose of the treatise is to open up important ecclesiological considerations for black theology, it will represent much of the writer's growing vision since he penned *A Black Political Theology*. It is hoped that it will draw an increasing number of gifted young black scholars, men and women, into a vital theological dialogue for the sake of the family and the church.

J.D.R.

CHAPTER I

An Introduction

I. THE PROBLEM

The black family and the black church have been studied by several black scholars of eminence. W. E. B. Du Bois,[1] E. Franklin Frazier,[2] and Andrew Billingsley[3] have written on these two primary institutions.

Other scholars have majored in the study of one of these two institutions. Robert Staples, for example, has studied well the black family.[4] Carter G. Woodson's study of the black church has not been surpassed.[5] C. Eric Lincoln has written on *The Black Church Since Frazier.*[6] Hart M. Nelsen and others, *The Black Church in America,* is mainly a sociological study of black churches.[7]

There is a need to continue to discuss family and church in the black experience in relation to each other. This should be done in regard to both their "symbolic" and "actual" relationship. On the one hand we need to explore the deeper meaning of church as family and family as church. On the other hand we need to explore the institutional importance of family and church in the black experience, considered separately and together. It is instructive that persons like Du Bois, Frazier, and Billingsley have seen the importance of each of these primary institutions, while black ministers and theologians have not thus far been as perceptive. The chal-

lenge now rests with our religious leadership to provide a
theological underpinning for the contributions made by col-
leagues in other disciplines. This treatise is a modest attempt
to meet this need.

The black family and the black church exist in a pluralistic
society in which the family is in serious trouble.[8] The White
House Conference on Families in 1980 attests to the seriousness of the problem. Because of the importance of the family
to any society, when the family is in trouble the nation is in
trouble.

In spite of the rash of evangelical piety, the churches in
this country do not enjoy the best of health. Preoccupied with
glory, with triumphalism, the church and its programs are
out of touch with the realities we must face in this period of
our history. The idols of science, technology, individualism,
and affluence have failed their devotees. It is becoming increasingly clear that the disciples of Jesus Christ must now
be prepared to take up a cross if they would be faithful to the
Lord of the church. In a world rampant with hunger, strife,
and many oppressions of the weak, there is a need to redis-
cover the cross and the practice of servanthood if the church
is not to lapse into a permanent state of apostasy.

Black families and churches are to be understood in the
context of American society. We are set in a situation of
pluralism. In spite of our peculiar history, blacks are affected
by the values that influence all other groups. It would be
unrealistic to ignore these facts. We shall be mindful of the
interaction and interdependence of blacks in the larger society, but our main focus will be upon the nature, destiny, and
mission of black families and churches in this country.

II. DEFINITIONS

We use the term "family" in a broad sense. While we are
aware that there is diversity within black families, it is the
common elements of the situation which we are prepared to
discuss. We are concerned about the nature and function of

the black family in our past, our present, and our future. Furthermore, what we discover in common is the basis for our togetherness, our peoplehood, which has been a persistent concern of ours. It should be added that we have an axiological interest in our consideration of the family. It is expected that we will through ethicotheological reflection point to what the black family *ought* to be and do.

We have in mind the family in its "extended" form. In the black community the family is not always limited by blood relationships. There is an informal adoption of children, and economic factors often bring people together who assume a symbolic kinship that may be rooted in deep affection. Families still exist that boast of intergenerational ties based upon blood relationships. These are more abundant in the rural South than in major urban centers. It is remarkable, however, how some individual families, which appear to be "nuclear," nourish and sustain these extended family ties. This is done through exchange visits over long distances on a regular basis. These families believe that the effort and the expense is justified, especially in benefits to their children. These extended family ties receive a real support from occasions like funerals, anniversaries, and family reunions, which bring large numbers of people of the same family tree together. We believe that this type of consciousness and deep sense of kinship should be encouraged and cultivated. The experience of belongingness of a people who are oppressed by racism leads to health, sanity, and wholeness. It is thus that we discover who we are, and thus that we are able to walk tall in spite of all we must endure.

There are two senses in which the word "church" is used here. We have in mind the Christian community associated with the revelation of God in Christ. We have in mind the life of the group that was formed about Jesus. The revelation of God in Christ is remembered in the church and is present wherever there is genuine Christian fellowship.[9] In the first instance, we view the church as a fellowship of believers in Christ, who take upon themselves the life-style and mission

of the crucified and resurrected Lord. The church is the
organ of the Spirit and the extension of the incarnation. It is
through repentance and faith that we are admitted to a relationship of grace within the body of Christ.

But the church is also an institution, an organization. As
such it is the instrument of the believing community. It is as
an institution that the church becomes a healing, socializing,
and humanizing agent. It is as an institution that the church
can become leaven, light, and salt. There is no necessary
conflict between the church's roles as organ of the spirit and
agent of liberation. In its priestly and prophetic work, the
church as organization becomes the agent that concretizes on
earth the will of the Lord of the church as a spirit-filled
fellowship. The church as organ has most to do with its
nature. The church as agent has most to do with mission. In
fact the two are inseparable. Only if we understand the nature
of the church are we able to participate fully in its mission
in the world.

What we have said about church and family has been thus
far descriptive and exploratory. It should suffice, however, to
provide some sense of how we perceive the nature and importance of the subject matter under investigation.

III. THE POINT OF VIEW

It has become increasingly clear that every writer should
clarify the point of view from which he writes. We believe
there is no one definitive theology of the black experience. It
is unfortunate that most observers of black theology consider
James H. Cone's thought as the norm for all black theology.
We have met this attitude among the most sympathetic white
theologians in this country, in West Germany, in Mexico,
and, somewhat unexpectedly, even among several African
theologians.

There is diversity within the unity of the black experience.
It is important to allow this diversity to inform our theologi-

cal reflection. It is only thus that the creativity of the several exponents of black theology can come to full expression. While Cone is to be honored as a pioneer theologian of the black experience, his program is not the norm or the last word. The subject matter of black religious experience, complicated by its African roots, is too vast for any one person to master. All of us have spent so much time with Western studies that we will not be able to complete our education in black sources in our lifetime. As practicing theologians, we must continue to keep abreast of general theological developments while we do our own creative work. This is why a team effort is needed in black theology. It may be that definitive studies will have to await the next generation of black scholars. What we wrote in 1973 about black theology as a theology "in the making" remains true.[10]

We welcome, therefore, the creative installments of all writers within our ranks. Where some are weak, others are strong; but we are brothers and sisters in a common cause. When only one black theologian is the recognized pacesetter, we are all vulnerable. If weaknesses are found in that one program, the entire effort can be dismissed. There are weaknesses in all of us, for we are all human, and humans are finite. The vital work we are doing requires many contributors, to supplement, strengthen, and correct one another. My message has been persistent: read all the black theologians. Here I can only repeat what I said earlier:

> We need unity without conformity to enable each black scholar to do what he can do best. We need serious and creative scholarship. Some will be interested in a Biblical theology; others will major in the historical or philosophical approaches. Some will major in methodology, others in content. . . . The problem of black suffering will challenge some. The nature and mission of the church will urge others on, while still others will pursue the Black Messiah. Black theology is a theology in the making and only the Lord of the Church knows at this moment the ultimate direction it will take.[11]

African theology is not determined by John Mbiti; feminine theology is not identical with the writings of Rosemary Ruether; neither is Latin-American liberation theology the sole product of Gustavo Gutiérrez. No one of them would make such a claim, and it is unfair to the serious efforts of these persons to identify the movements they represent with their contributions. The point applies pertinently to the undue burden placed upon James H. Cone. I am encouraged by recent collections of essays in French, Italian, and Dutch which have recognized most of the major writers in the field. Allan A. Boesak, a black South African theologian, in his *Farewell to Innocence,* has pointed in a significant direction. While devoting much of his attention to James Cone's writings, he has done justice to the major literature in the field.[12] Several black theologians have been impartial and fair, including Cecil Cone, James Cone's brother. James Cone himself has entered into discussion with other black theologians in *God of the Oppressed.*[13] Still, many white theologians, who express deep concern for issues raised in black theology, respond primarily to Cone. Many vigorously attack some aspect of Cone's program with which other black theologians do not agree, and believe they have dealt with black theology. Examples would be the "liberation-oppression" formula and the advocacy of violence. One wonders if these writers are under the control of a preconscious form of racism. In evaluating other theological movements they do not usually operate in this manner.

In this book, we will not move in the shadow of any other black theologian. Our effort will be to think out of our own encounter with life, out of our own spiritual and intellectual pilgrimage, and as a member of a family and a church within the black experience. We will not be limited by the black experience, but will move within and without where necessary. Our anchor, however, will be within this ethnic setting. Black sources will be used and we will interact critically with several black writers, past and present. We will take our

African roots seriously. Euro-American and Third World materials will be used freely but not uncritically. All materials and ideas will be used descriptively and we refuse to place a greater value on Western sources than on any others. We categorically reject the colonization of the mind as well as the political domination of the West in reference to the rest of humankind. We shall strive to be human in our concern for the rights of women and will attempt to avoid male-dominated language where this is possible. We are mindful of a network of oppression based upon race, sex, and class, and we endorse the right of all humans to be free and equal. At the same time our special focus is upon race as a form of oppression. Our particular context is the spiritual and cultural heritage of Afro-Americans.

IV. METHODOLOGY

Nathan Hare, founding editor of *The Black Scholar,* has said that America is like a giant octopus with a body and many tentacles. The Afro-American, Hare notes, lives inside the body; Third World societies encounter only the tentacles. Black Americans, then, are able to deliver the most decisive blows to make the system more humane. This is a good analogy with which to start our discussion on methodology in black theology.

Black theology is duty bound to take Africa seriously. This consideration must not be restricted to "Christian church" Africa, but must include traditional Africa as well. A theological hermeneutic adequate for the task of interpreting the black religious experience must include more than any christological proposal thus far formulated in Western theology.

In the spirit of Hare's analogy, black theologians have a major responsibility in providing a bridge between Western and Third World theologies. Our roots are in Africa and yet we are Americans. This may not have been our choice, but it is our destiny. The Afro-American is African and American at the same time. In contradistinction to Africans who visit here, we are not *in* but *of* this country. Therefore we are in a unique position to provide two-way conversation between Third World theologians and Euro-American theologians. We will not be able to facilitate this dialogue, however, unless we are open to thought structures and religious traditions that differ from those of the West. Levi A. Nwachuku writes that Africa is "the last open frontier of big power politics."[14] The same may be said for theology. It is the responsibility of black theologians to open up this frontier. To this end we need a proper hermeneutic.

A. A Comprehensive View of Revelation

Karl Barth was a pacesetter in Euro-American theology for a half century. My recent visit to West German theological schools has confirmed that his thought is still alive and well in West German theological circles. Many outstanding contemporary theologians take their departure from Barth. As one youthful theologian put it, "One must know Barth well, even if it is to get rid of him." After discussions with several students and admirers of Barth, including Eberhard Jüngel of Tübingen, it is my judgment that Karl Barth is greatly responsible for the decline in the study of non-Western religions. It is essential that we allow Barth to speak for himself. Barth writes:

> Revelation does not link up with a human religion which is already present and practised. It contradicts it, just as religion previously contradicted revelation. It displaces it, just as religion previously displaced revelation.[15]

This exclusive view of revelation is buttressed by his christocentrism, which is also exclusive. Without Jesus Christ there would be no Christian religion. Like other religions, it would be merely human religion—a form of idolatry and self-righteousness. Barth writes:

> The name of Jesus Christ alone has created the Christian
> gion. . . . Because it was and is and shall be through the n[a]
> of Jesus Christ, it was and is and shall be the true religion.

The revelation of God is limited to Christianity, according
to Barth. The locus of revelation is Jesus Christ. Barth's
discussion of Amida-Buddha and grace in the Japanese Bud-
dhism of Shinran and in Indian Bhakti religion does not
improve the impression that he has his mind made up
and that he introduces these religions mainly to prove his
point.[17]

According to Cone, Jesus Christ is the one whom black
people have met in the historical struggle of freedom.[18] He
now observes that black people have a tradition that goes
back to Africa and its traditional religions.[19] Africans
brought with them their stories and combined them with the
Christian story.[20] Christ is the "otherness" in the black experience that makes possible the affirmation of black humanity
in an inhuman situation.[21] When Cone asserts that Jesus is
black because he was a Jew, he is concerned about Jesus'
identification with the poor for their liberation. Blackness,
however, limited to the "social existence" of Afro-Americans, does not scratch the surface of poverty among humans.
Does he wish to expand blackness to include all the poor? Is
his formula of oppression/liberation adequate to open up a
meaningful discussion with traditional African religions?
Cone rightly observes that "blackness as a christological title
may not be appropriate in the distant future or even in every
human context in our present."[22] He explains:

> The validity of any christological title in any period of history
> is not decided by its universality but by this: whether in the
> particularity of its time it points to God's universal will to liber-
> ate particular oppressed people from inhumanity.[23]

Cone wants to affirm that Christ is literally and symboli-
cally black in America.[24] But I shudder when he adds, "Indeed, if Christ is not *truly* black, then the historical Jesus
lied."[25] I share his concern that the gospel be made concrete

with reference to a particular people. He broadens his perspective as he adds:

> The transcendent . . . God has not ever, no not ever, left the
> oppressed alone in struggle. He was with them in Pharaoh's
> Egypt, He is with them in America, Africa, Latin America, and
> He will come in the end time to consummate fully their free-
> dom.[26]

In a recent essay Cone has expressed an openness to the
thought of Martin Luther King, to Marxism, and to other
theologies of liberation. He urges us "to move beyond a mere
reaction to white racism in America and begin to extend our
vision . . . to the whole inhabited earth."[27] But the new range
of vision seems still to be political only. This is just not
sufficient. How will he deal with cultural and historical aspects of the African/Afro-American connection? How will
he expand his christological proposal, in which his entire
program is centered, to encounter the Africanization of theology? While the political focus of Cone's theology makes
direct contact with racist oppression in South Africa, it does
not move easily into dialogue with postcolonial African peoples who face more cultural and psychological types of crises.
An adequate theological method must be sought which will
create fruitful dialogue between all peoples of African descent.

Charles Long, a black historian of religion, approaches the
problem of the relation of black religious experience to black
theology and also the relation of African traditional religion
to African Christian theology. Long views the thought structures of theology as too limited to resolve this problem. Long
is reacting, I believe, to the limits imposed by Cone and
similar theologians. The discussion between Long and Cone
has thus far been a "misplaced debate" simply because theology and history of religions are opposed to each other.[28] The
way forward for both black scholars and Africans is to allow
these two disciplines to supplement each other.

Long wants us to consider the elements of religious experience as phenomena. He would describe the "specifically religious elements in the religion of black Americans."[29] It is his view that the approach of the social sciences and theology cannot do this.[30] He goes on to explain what he finds: (1) Africa as a historical reality and religious image, (2) the involuntary presence of the black community in America, and (3) the experience and symbol of God.[31] Cone's summary of Long's intention appears accurate and I repeat it here:

> He contended that Christianity generally and theology in particular are too limited for dealing with what he calls "opacity" of the religious symbol in the African and black communities. He used the opaque symbol in contrast to Paul Tillich's understanding of the transparent symbol, or the Western European's interpretation of that ideological age which justified colonialism and Western progressivism, the Enlightenment. Thus he contended that the fundamental question is whether there does exist a symbol of the opaque of the Black that is creative, beneficial, universal, and whether we as a people are called upon to give witness for its meaning for the sake of all humanity.[32]

I believe Long is on a significant trail, but I do not desire to consider the Christian revelation as excess baggage. On the other hand, it will not be possible to join him in this quest if one draws the hermeneutical circle of revelation as small as Cone does. Somehow we must bring the descriptive-phenomenological approach of Long and the faith-revelation approach of Cone together. Black theology can be critical and confessional at the same time. This will be the burden of our effort. My own position has been discussed elsewhere.[33] But in order to bring this section to a close I quote the following conclusions:

> The black theologian stands in a circle of faith not merely as a believer, but also as an interpreter of faith for a believing community. He is seeking a way to enter into a climate of creative encounter and dialogue with religionists at home and abroad who share a common religious and cultural heritage without

surrendering his own affirmation of faith. . . . The God of such a theology of religions must be one who unveils His mind, will and purpose in all creation, in all history and among all peoples even though He may yet be known most completely through the Incarnation.[34]

B. Symbolic Thinking

Amos N. Wilder writes on theology and the religious imagination in his *Theopoetic.*[35] He reminds us that religious communication must overcome "a long addiction to the discursive, the rationalistic, and the prosaic."[36] Wilder writes:

> Before the message there must be the vision, before the sermon the hymn, before the prose the poem. . . . The structures of faith and confession have always rested on hierophanies and images.[37]

Wilder argues for the theopoetic. In any situation theology should relate to philosophical ideas, but it also should use symbolic life and creative impulses. Theology, according to Wilder, properly takes the form of clear thinking about God, the faith, and the world. At the same time it has a basic substratum of imaginative grasp on reality and experience. Wilder recalls:

> The thought of Aquinas was indebted to the visionary structures that inspired Dante, as that of Augustine was to those that inspired Neo-Platonism. There is a correspondence between Milton's *De Doctrina Christiana* and his *Paradise Lost.*[38]

Wilder's avowed purpose is to make theology more cogent as it redefines itself in relation to the dominant myths, dreams, and images of the age. He does not intend that the gospel is to be conformed to the world and its ideologies. The theologian should be able to identify the sensibility of the day, even though he is sure of the convictions upon which he or she stands.[39]

The value of Wilder's discussion for our purpose is that he reminds us of the possibility of supplementing the knowledge of faith we gain through discursive reasoning through the religious imagination. His discourse on "theopoetic" opens up the possibility of thinking theologically by means of symbols, myths, and metaphors.

My discovery of Pascal's "reasons of the heart" years ago opened up a new possibility for thought. Pascal convinced me that on the deeper levels of experience there are truths more profound than those gained through logic. Pascal uses "reasons" in a double sense when he speaks of the "reasons of the heart which reason cannot comprehend." When Pascal speaks of reason, *la superbe raison,* he means pure reason or discourse, the typical reasoning of the dogmatist. Such reason is instrumental. He does not discuss it but ascribes its limits. Such reason is slow to act and often fails for lack of necessary evidence or facts, while feeling is instant and always ready to act. Feeling and faith belong together. The heart feels God and not reason. That is the meaning of faith.

The heart as Pascal uses it has Hebraic overtones and is conceived as being at the center of the human personality. The heart includes thought, feeling, and will and represents the whole personality in its innermost being. It integrates every energy in the service of a cause to which one owes allegiance. Reason cannot command our complete loyalty, and thus ultimate things are known by the heart. Pascal does not mean that faith is merely a matter of feeling. Intuition surpasses reason in its ability to grasp truth as a whole. The heart does not effect proofs, but grasps their significance and effects their synthesis. Reason is full of contradictions and in the end must surrender to a higher type of knowledge.[40] Paul Tillich is correct, I believe, as he observes of Pascal: "The 'reasons of the heart' are the structures of aesthetic and communal experience (beauty and love); the reason 'which cannot comprehend them' is technical reason."[41] Studies in Pascal as well as Kierkegaard and other existentialists have opened up my mind to creative ways of thinking.

Existential thinkers explored the use of literature as a means of communication. They also made creative use of the unconscious in their search for the deeper meaning of human existence. In addition, studies in Neoplatonism, mysticism, and Eastern religions have all prepared my mind and spirit for a break with Western substance metaphysics as the only way to truth.[42] I do not find process thought, with its Whiteheadian metaphysics, to be the proper alternative to the Platonic-Aristotelian tradition. It is not merely because process thought is also Western, it is rather because it does not carry the freight that needs to be carried by the theological mission I have in mind. We have only opened up the possibility for symbolic thinking here, but the matter will be pursued later as we work out our understanding of the family and church in the black experience.

CHAPTER II

The Family
in the
Black Experience

Psychology Today devoted its May 1977 issue to "The American Family in Trouble." Walter F. Mondale provided the lead article, in which he cited alarming increases in juvenile crime, illegitimacy, suicide among the young, and abuse of children by their parents or guardians.[1] Urie Bronfenbrenner, Susan Byrne, and others wrote about the erosion of family life and programs that often hinder rather than help.[2] The Family Union on the Lower East Side of Manhattan is presented as having a program that "really works." Its purpose is to prevent the breakup of families by linking up families in need with the agencies which provide the proper help.[3]

A year later, *Newsweek* provided a special report, "Saving the Family," which included a section on the "fresh trials" of the black family.[4] The family in general, and the black family in particular, must be given much study and attention if our nation is to survive a serious world crisis. The *Newsweek* report provides a look at alternative groups that would substitute for families: e.g., "communes," but most mature conclusions point to the need to rescue and strengthen traditional families.[5]

I. THE BLACK FAMILY IN TROUBLE

In 1965, President Lyndon B. Johnson gave a speech at
Howard University. The speech, drafted by Richard N.
Goodwin and Daniel Patrick Moynihan, was entitled "To
Fulfill These Rights." It was based in part on the controversial Moynihan Report on black families. Moynihan had in
essence ascribed the "pathology" of the black family to its
"matriarchy" in a society which is predominantly "patriar-
chial."[6] Quoting from the black sociologist E. Franklin
Frazier, Moynihan observed that middle-class black families
are often headed by men, they are reduced in size, and they
seek to preserve the gains they have made. But the "pathology" is rampant in lower-class families. It is obvious why
President Johnson carried the gist of this study to Howard
University, the most influential black institution of higher
education in the nation. This commencement address could
reach, not just the young, but alumni, parents, and friends
assembled from all over this country and much of the Third
World.

President Johnson's speech was well balanced. It dealt
with many basic problems in the area of human rights. There
is a section, however, on the black family and its breakdown,
which obviously reflects the Moynihan Report. Johnson
speaks of the oppression and persecution of the black male.
His dignity has been assaulted and with this his ability to
provide for his family. The President says: "Only a minority,
less than half, of all Negro children reach the age of 18
having lived all their lives with both of their parents."[7]

The President next spoke decisive words that we cannot
ignore:

> The family is the cornerstone of our society. More than any other
> force it shapes the attitudes, the hopes, the ambitions, and the
> values of the child. When the family collapses it is the children
> that are usually damaged. When it happens on a massive scale
> the community itself is crippled. Unless we work to strengthen
> the family, to create conditions under which most parents will

stay together, all the rest: schools and playgrounds, public assistance and private concern, will never be enough to cut completely the circle to despair and deprivation.[8]

The Moynihan Report measured such things as unemployment, median income, illegitimacy, female-headed households, children on welfare, and children under eighteen living with both parents. If these measurements were taken today the picture would be even worse.[9] There are now more middle-class families, but there are an increasing number of female-headed families. More black children are born out of wedlock, often to girls still in their teens. More black heads of households are without jobs.

It was not the facts, but the way the facts were interpreted, that gave rise to the rigorous criticism of this report. In essence, Moynihan asserted that the sickness of the black family was the cause of the deterioration of the black community. He should rather have stressed the oppression which has been so destructive to black families. While we cannot ignore the present crisis in the black family, we must deal with the root cause and not merely with symptoms if we are to strengthen black families.

It is perhaps unfortunate that this report was released into the headwinds of black pride. Moynihan, as Assistant Secretary of Labor, hoped that his findings would promote long-range policies designed to improve employment opportunities and encourage welfare programs. His conclusions and the yardstick he used to describe the "pathology" of the black family has been attacked by sociologists, black and white. Slavery is the real backdrop for single-parent, female-headed families.

Revisionists like Andrew Billingsley and Robert B. Hill have been forceful in finding the strengths of black families in the "extended family" pattern among blacks. Black families, they hold, survived their long journey from Africa to urban America by developing characteristic strengths—chiefly a sense of extended family to provide support and

nurture during crisis or parental absence. Babies born out of
wedlock were kept in the family. Today 90 percent of such
children are still reared by parents or relatives. This is to be
compared with 33 percent of illegitimate white babies kept in
the home. Money, food, and child care are shared among
kinfolk, to the point of informal adoption of children for
periods of time.[10] This is a way of arguing that in an oppressive racist society, black families have developed coping
mechanisms not merely to survive, but to maintain some
measure of sanity and health.

But the warning of Howard University sociologist Har-
riette McAdoo is to be heeded. She indicates that we should
not romanticize the strengths of black families out of context.
We have survived, she agrees, in the face of real and threaten-
ing problems. The fact remains, however, that the strain
upon the black family structures is increasing. The statistics
are alarming regarding negative factors. This means that
within the not too distant future we may find that the black
family is overwhelmed by these massive problems.[11] Both
McAdoo and Billingsley hold that if black families are provided for, they will stabilize themselves. In fact, the support
system built into the black extended family should be considered for mainstream families. What black families need are
jobs, homes, and education, to pull them out of their present
slump.[12] It is the responsibility of black theologians to remind
black families of the moral and spiritual resources inherent
in the black family tradition, without which we may not
survive.

The black family is an institution of great value to black
people. It must not only survive, it must prevail. But the
black family is in serious trouble. I am not ready to preach
a eulogy at its graveside; nor am I as optimistic as some black
sociologists seem to be. It does not help to observe that white
families also are being torn apart by such things as sexual
permissiveness, women's liberation, and the like.[13] With all
due respect to Margaret Mead, I am not convinced of her

prophecy that "in the end, it will be the family way of life that will persevere."[14] Something happens to a people when you tamper with healthy families. The Chinese example should give us pause.

The present government of China in the name of social betterment has uprooted an ancient family system that cemented Chinese society for thousands of years. The result is as follows:

> The forced separations have brought heartbreak, corruption and adultery. They have made life nerve-racking and sometimes politically dangerous.[15]

Changes in which husbands and wives and children are uprooted, play havoc with the upbringing of children and destroy the intergenerational sense of kinship. While all this is done in the name of being unselfish for the cause of the motherland, there seem to be cracks in the social system, causing real alarm.[16] Whatever the gains resulting from the new arrangements, the destruction of a time-honored family system with its built-in kinship loyalties and moral values is bound to be costly. The attempt to restore Confucius to a place of honor may indicate a felt need to recapture some of the values of the traditional family system.

Blows to the black family, suffered involuntarily in the United States, create a similar need to restore the family to the place it has in traditional Africa. This we must do if we are to be a united and strong people—if we are to find our way to a healthy and whole existence. The black family is a dike against the oppressive system as well as a group bound together by blood and other kinship ties. Nathan Hare is correct when he asserts that we must deal with the cause of the ills of the black family in the system. But we must face head on the real problems of black families, whether internal or external, psychological, sociological or economic, and seek to find solutions to those problems.[17]

Hare laments that black critics of Moynihan largely wrote

off his statistical findings involving the relationship between racial and economic oppression and black family decay. "These correlations were among the highest yet known to behavioral and social sciences."[18]

Why did not black scholars examine the figures? Hare's explanation is interesting. He writes:

> Their over-reaction to Moynihan's interpretation, coming as it did in 1965 at the twilight of the era of black ultra-assimilationism, was motivated in part by collective feelings of inferiority. These pangs of inferiority gave rise among Black intellectuals . . . to a pathetic preoccupation with "petty defenses" of the Black race—i.e., to deny the pathology of oppression, in a desperate attempt to spotlight hard-earned "strengths" in the search for white recognition.[19]

Hare notes, however, that self-affirmation as a counter response to oppression is too psychogenic to constitute the most effective approach to social change, let alone the only one.[20] Even if Hare explains in part the initial response of black scholars to the Moynihan Report, he does not explain such important writers as Andrew Billingsley and Herbert Hill, whose writings seem to emerge clearly out of black pride and power.

Hare makes a frontal attack upon the "strength-of-black-families school." The black family with a female at the head is the result of black oppression in the United States instead of a genuine and deliberately chosen alternative form. Hare writes that black sociologists led the black movement away from an attack on the suffering of blacks in their family situation. "In the name of false pride, they pretend that all is well with the Black family in America, despite our recognized economic, educational, and political deprivation."[21]

This line of thought minimizes the psychological effects of the black male's unemployment and the social destruction in the black family by the siphoning off of the black male into the labor market, prisons, or military camps.

Hare does not view the black matriarchy as acceptable to blacks. It cannot become a positive reality for family members in our urban centers. The black matriarchy is a myth, Hare argues, both because it is unacceptable to blacks and because it is not viable. He has harsh words for those who approve the black matriarchy when the black male needs to be upgraded. Hare writes: "These intellectuals turned their backs on Black reconstruction and the belated restructuring of the Black family as a springboard, or at least a link in the chain of struggle for Black socio-economic elevation. Thus, we sit back and cheerfully allow the Black male's participation in the labor force . . . to relentlessly deteriorate. Predictably, the proportion of Black females doomed to head family groups swells accordingly."[22]

Meanwhile these intellectuals even extol the existing situation:

> The female-headed family and the extended maternal family (where the unwed, the deserted or divorced young mother and/or her children must live with the maternal grandmother) also increase.[23]

In these last observations Hare comes close to the concerns of those who minister to black families in trouble. The solution will involve, as Hare suggests, an assessment of "positives" and "negatives."[24] While we celebrate the "resiliency" of black families against great odds, we must go to work on real problems that afflict black families from within and from without. Hare has a doctorate in both sociology and psychology. It is as psychologist that he is perhaps best able to expose the weaknesses of the sociologists who mainly make up the strength-of-black-families school. While I do not reject all that this school has to offer, I am grateful to Hare for pointing to these deficiencies.[25] The black theologian should take such studies seriously while making his own distinctive contribution to the Christian understanding of our personal and group life.

II. THE BLACK FAMILY IN HISTORY

Any breakthrough in our understanding of the black family must begin with the African experience. Alex Haley's *Roots* affords a perspective on the social history of the black family. His work is the saga of his own family, which goes back to 1750 in an African village.[26] Haley does not claim to be a disciplined scholar in anthropology or sociology, but he tells his family story as a journalist. He provides a framework in which the plight of the black family in the United States may be discussed. Most black families, like Haley's, began somewhere in West Africa.

Africa cherishes strong extended families. The family system with its ancestor cult is at the heart of religion and social organization. It is not true that Africans, who were brought to this country in chains, did not have strong families. The fact is that slavery uprooted Africans from a long history of strong family and community life. Their family system was different from that of their captors, but it was just as viable.

Billingsley describes African family life in some detail. First, marriage was a relationship which involved more than the couple and their two families. It involved a network of extended kinship with considerable influence and responsibility for the marriage and the well-being of a new family. Marriage could neither be entered into nor abandoned without community support. Second, pre-European African marriage was anchored in a long history of tribal tradition, ritual, custom, and law. Third, family life was highly articulated with the rest of society. The family was an economic and a religious unit and, through its ties with the wider kinship circles, was also a political unit. The family of Africa was central to its culture and brought great influence to bear upon personal life.[27]

Men are assigned a decisive role in the African family and society. This strong masculine position was balanced by a substantial role for women. Male authority is limited by custom and tradition. Children receive care and protection from mother and father, but from a wider kinship group as well. There were three basic patterns of descent or kinship ties in Africa. The most common was the patrilineal, in which kinship ties are traced through the father's side of the family. Next was the matrilineal, in which kinship was reckoned through the mother's side of the family. A third pattern, at the present, is that of double descent. This is infrequently found and mainly in the southern portion of the continent. This pattern, well recognized in the United States, was virtually unknown in the part of West Africa from which American blacks came.[28] West Africans had a highly complex civilization. Their patterns of family life were closely knit, well organized, highly articulated with kin and community, and highly functional for the economic, social, and psychological life of the people.[29]

We will not pursue the African roots of the black family further at this time. Our purpose has been to introduce the extended model of the family and to indicate the African background to this family pattern. By presenting this account of the African family, we are able to appreciate the disruption the slave system brought in the lives of black families.

III. SLAVERY AND THE BLACK FAMILY

Nathan Glazer raises the cardinal question regarding slavery: "Why was American slavery the most awful the world has ever known?"[30] It was profoundly different from and, in its effects on families, worse than any recorded servitude, ancient or modern. Alexis de Tocqueville noted this in the 1830's. Frank Tannenbaum has pointed out the differences between slavery in the United States and Brazil. In essence the slave in Brazil had a place in the social hierarchy—it was the lowest place, but still the slave was a human being. In contrast, in the United States, the slave was considered as chattel.

To be quite specific Glazer notes:

In Brazil, the slave had many more rights than in the United States: he could legally marry . . . be baptized and become a member of the Catholic Church, his family could not be broken up for sale, and he had many days on which he could either rest or earn money to buy his freedom. The government encouraged manumission, and the freedom of infants could often be purchased for a small sum at the baptismal font.[31]

In short, the Brazilian slave was treated as a human being, though as one different and inferior in reference to the master.

Slavery in the United States was radically different. The slave was removed from the protection of organized society. The humanity of the slave was disregarded by sacred and secular institutions. He or she was cut off from the past and without hope for the future. Children could be sold, marriage was not recognized, women could be isolated or sold at will. The slave could not, by law, be taught to read or write. Religion could not be practiced without the permission of the master. Slaves were forbidden to congregate except in the presence of whites. Even if a master wanted to free a slave, every legal means was used to prevent this. Stanley M. Elkins has compared United States slavery to internment in Nazi concentration camps.[32] Both are seen as closed systems. The intention was to reduce the slave to childishness, to absolute obedience and total dependence. This practice had a devastating impact on black households. The result was often a fatherless, matrifocal pattern of family life.

Eugene D. Genovese's work[33] would lead one to the belief that slavery was quite humane, all things being considered. The facts are that slavery was cruel and inhuman. It began as early as 1619 and lasted until the 1860's. It disrupted the cultural life of those Africans who were enslaved. It threw their history into discontinuity and dealt such a terrible blow to family life, the primary unit of social organization, that we are still unsettled.

Slaves were brought involuntarily to a strange society in

which their historical norms, values, and ways of life were unfamilar and unacceptable. They came from different tribes with diverse languages, cultures, and traditions. They came without their families and often without females. They came in chains. Furthermore, even if they could adapt to the new culture, they were not free to engage in the ordinary process of acculturation as European immigrants. They were cut off from their native culture without being permitted to develop and assimilate a new one. In this manner black slaves in the United States—people who had been free, independent human beings with a strong family support system—were converted in a matter of months into property. Lerone Bennett describes the tragedy thus: "Slavery was a black man who stepped out of his hut . . . for a breath of fresh air and ended up ten months later in Georgia with bruises on his back and a brand on his chest."[34]

The slave system in the United States was especially vicious in regard to family life. The family was broken up at the very beginning of the slave trade in the manner in which the slaves were gathered, the disregard the captors showed for family and kinship ties, the preference they showed for selecting young men in the prime of life, the lack of black females for a long period of time, and the inhuman conditions under which slaves were quartered, worked, and treated.

There was also an absence of legal foundation, sanction, and protection of marriage as an institution among slaves. Slave women were exploited by white owners, overseers, and their sons, for pleasure and profit. A role for the black man as husband and father was systematically denied. Families were willfully separated by selling members to different plantations. In a word, the black family had no physical, psychological, social, or economic protection. This crippled individuals, families—a whole people. The consequences of this, "America's National Sin," upon generations of blacks are direct and insidious. The "lengthening shadow of slavery" still hovers over the black family. Nor has society made any massive effort to undo the damage that slavery inflicted upon black families. In fact, explicit results of slavery still exist. We shall not be able to correct this evil until the cause behind the present plight of the black family is recognized.[35]

Emancipation was a difficult experience for ex-slaves. Blacks were simply turned out into the world ill prepared to shift for themselves. Some left the plantation immediately, some changed their names, but some, especially older house servants, were reluctant to leave. As the plantation system was swept away, many became refugees. In these unsettled times the strong bond between parents and children as well as men and women was manifest. Many blacks sought to trace missing members of their families and there were many family reunions.[36] E. Franklin Frazier writes:

> The strong attachment which . . . mothers showed for their children during the crisis of emancipation could be matched with instances of deep affection between husbands and wives and between children and their parents.[37]

Promiscuous sexual relations and constant changing of spouses became the rule with the demoralized elements in the freed black population. Some of the confusion in marital relations can be traced to the forced separation of husbands and wives during slavery and the general social disorganization of the times. Northern missionaries were hard put to improve the morals of the newly liberated slaves.[38] The confusion was brought to light when ex-slaves decided to enter into formal marriage. Some women who had lived with men desired to consecrate and legalize their marriage. Often the men desired other women. There even seemed to be a superstition against formal marriage. Some former slaves were forced to get married. Others were pleased to confirm a union based upon genuine love over a long period of time.[39] When the bonds of sympathy and affection between members of these families were strong enough to remain unbroken, the struggle for existence tended to strengthen family ties.[40] Frazier writes:

Where families had developed a fair degree of organization during slavery, the male head assumed responsibility for their support. In fact, the severe hardships became a test of strength of
family ties.[41]

Frazier drew the following conclusions from his study of
the family conditions among blacks after emancipation:
First, the families that had achieved a fair degree of organization during slavery made the transition without much distur-
bance to the routine of living. In these families the authority
of the father was firmly established and the woman in the role
of mother and wife fitted into the pattern of the patriarchal
household. The father also assumed the status of the chief,
if not the sole, breadwinner. It was often done through ac-
quiring land and through this means consolidating the common interests of the family. Second, the loose ties that had
held men and women together in a nominal marriage relation
during slavery broke easily during the crises of emancipation.
When this happened, the men cut themselves loose from all
family ties and joined the great body of homeless men wan-
dering about the country in search of work and new experiences. Some women, usually those without children, followed
the same course. But more often the woman with family ties,
whether she had been without a husband during slavery or
was deserted when freedom came, became responsible for the
maintenance of the family group. Motherhood outside of
institutional control became the lot of a large group of black
women.[42] Unhappily this is still too often the case.[43]

The end of slavery did not solve the problems of blacks.
They were free, but free to die of starvation and illness. Many
died; destitution and disease were rampant. The survival of
blacks can be attributed only to the resiliency of the human
spirit. The suggestion that blacks be given forty acres and a
mule fell on deaf ears. The response to the needs of blacks
was too limited and temporary. The Freedmen's Bureau, a
national social welfare program, operated only six years with
limited funds. It faced apathy in the North and hostility in

the South. It strove to feed and shelter ex-slaves and poor whites, and to establish hospitals and schools. It was administered with imagination and courage and did a great job under these circumstances.

All efforts to help the blacks faced countermeasures. Violence caused the Fourteenth and Fifteenth Amendments to be passed. Federal enforcement laws were inadequate, especially when enforcement was in the South. Blacks would not vote if this meant losing their jobs, even their lives. Members of the Klan supervised the elections. The South was being left to its own devices. The Confederates enjoyed enormous prestige. They seized political and economic power. But they would also shoot or hang a black if this were needed to have their way. They reduced the black voters to a trickle by hook or crook. They would withdraw tax funds to tone down radical reconstruction. They used any and all methods to destroy radical reconstruction and their efforts succeeded.

We will treat the urbanization of blacks and the impact of this process upon family life later on in our study. At this time we will attempt to assess the status of black family life through slavery and the decade immediately after. Frazier indicates that some slaves retained certain aspects of African culture, but as each generation passed they lived with a fading memory. More and more, their personalities reflected the role which they acquired in the plantation economy.

Many of the sexual taboos and restraints imposed by original African cultures were lost. The behavior of the slaves was subject at first only to the control of the slave masters and the wishes of those selected for mates. Slaves were only "animate tools"—instruments of production. Brute force was relied upon as the chief means of control. Sexual relations were likely to be dissociated, on the whole, from human sentiments and feelings.[44] For instance, masters had sexual relations freely with their own slave daughters. They would willingly sell their own slave children to other masters. Black men stood by helplessly and witnessed their wives and daughters being violated by slave masters and their sons.

But where slavery became a settled way of life the slaves did select affectionately their own mates. If opportunity afforded, they developed strong attachments. They were limited in these unions by the social controls operative in the plantation system. Within the slave community, the master held an important position and played a dominant role in family groupings. Mothers had a fierce attachment to their children. On the whole, the slave family developed as a natural organization, based upon the spontaneous feelings of affection and natural sympathies resulting from the association of family members in the same household. There were many fathers who held an emotional and responsible attachment to their wives and children. This was never easy because the master had the power of male dominance over all women.

The slave mother was protectress of the master's children. Thus the tradition which is a paradox in the slave system emerged. The black "mammy" became the foster parent of the slave master. This is to be viewed together with the incessant cohabitation of the men of the white race with black women in the slave system. This practice was so extensive that to a great extent it nullified monogamy.

The result of this one-way mixing of blood was a mulatto group which became a channel by means of which the ideals, customs, and mores of the whites were mediated to the blacks. There were often situations where they could assimilate the culture of whites. These mixed-bloods had the opportunity of being servants in the master's house and sometimes they were educated by the white forebear. The key seems to have been how well the master thought of the slave mother of these half-breeds. But, although many of the persons of mixed blood were poor and degraded, they picked up attitudes about a more stable form of family life. Thus after the Civil War family traditions soon became firmly established among this class.

Emancipation destroyed the *modus vivendi* established between the races during slavery. The many intimate and sympathetic ties between the races were severed. Blacks began to build their own institutions by imitation of white culture and through education. Some became landowners, but most became sharecroppers and tenants. They were a free but landless people. A black folk culture developed which had its peculiar social organization and values. The maternal family continued on a large scale. Illegitimacy is widespread in rural communities. But illegitimacy does not disrupt the family organization. Children born out of wedlock are absorbed into a larger family circle. Family stability and black social organization has usually been tied to the fortunes of southern agriculture. Up until the beginning of the present century many ambitious and energetic former slaves and their descendants have sought education and have bought property. In these instances the father and/or husband seems to be more in the center of the family as an established authority figure. These families sprang from the more stable, reliable, and intelligent elements from the former slave population.[45] Frazier writes:

> The emergence of this class of families from the mass of the Negro population has created small nuclei of stable families with conventional standards of sexual morality all over the South. Although culturally these families may be distinguished from those of free ancestry, they have intermarried from time to time with the latter families. These families represent the highest development of Negro family life up to the opening of the present century.[46]

It should be obvious from this survey of the turbulent experience of blacks in slavery that family life has been severely scarred by this tragic experience. As ugly and as painful as a restating of this experience has been, it is necessary to retrace the pilgrimage of the black family in order to understand the problems and deal with the needs of black persons and families in our ministry today and tomorrow. Our next effort will be to trace the black church experience in a similar manner before we treat family and church together in the black experience.

CHAPTER III

The Church
in the
Black Experience

The selection of the "church" within the black experience limits the focus of our intention. We might have treated Jewish and Islamic religious institutions as well. However, we are concerned mainly with the church as a historic institution within the black experience. Black religious experience in general is the matrix out of which the black church tradition comes. Like the family, black religious experience has its roots in Africa. Any in-depth study of the black church tradition will of necessity begin with African traditional religion.

I. THE AFRICAN BACKGROUND
IN THE BLACK CHURCH TRADITION

Henry H. Mitchell has provided a significant document which links the black church tradition with West Africa. Mitchell's book is entitled *Black Belief*. He focuses upon "Folk Beliefs of Blacks," but in fact he is primarily concerned with the black Christian's appropriation of this African/Afro-American religious tradition. Mitchell writes:

> The folk religion of the masses of black Americans is clearly an adaptation of the African—traditional—religion base brought over by the various West Africans who were pressed into slavery.[1]

Mitchell makes the important point that slavery struck a terrible blow to the African world view and value systems. I believe he is correct in assuming that the African influence has survived in spite of slavery and other forms of oppression blacks have undergone and are undergoing in the United States. He writes:

> I am now convinced that the slavocracy failed to erase African culture, but slowly succeeded in getting Blacks to be ashamed of it. The result was that even though we Blacks continued to use and adapt our own heritage, we eventually dropped many aspects of it.[2]

Slavery did strike a powerful blow at these survivals, and we are still reeling from its impact. But we move forward with the assumption that black scholarship supported by recent ethnological studies in Africa by African and/or black scholars has provided sufficient evidence for us to proceed with the assurance that "Africanisms" are present in Afro-American culture, including religious experience.[3]

John W. Blassingame agrees with Gayraud Wilmore's proposal that the most important inheritance of black Americans from Africa is not musical or rhythmic, but is in the nature of philosophy, world view, and values, in a word, religion.[4] Blassingame, an authority on the slave community, provides this comment:

> The similarities between many European and African cultural elements enabled the slave to continue to engage in many traditional activities or to create a synthesis of European and African cultures. In the process of acculturation the slaves made European forms serve African functions. An example of this is religion. . . . Christian forms were so similar to African religious patterns that it was relatively easy for the early slaves to incorporate them with their traditional practices and beliefs. In America, Jehovah replaced Creator, and Jesus replaced the Holy Ghost, and the Saints replaced all the lesser gods. . . . After a few generations, the slaves forgot the African deities

represented by the Judeo-Christian gods, but in many other facets of their religious services they retained many African elements.[5]

Henry Mitchell explains the obvious openness of blacks to the Christian faith by a strong religious bent in their heritage. Slaves took the initiative to translate their African beliefs into English and Christian terms. They sorted through the Bible and selected the ideas useful to them in view of their slave experience. By the time the masters were willing to concede souls to the slaves, satisfied that the Christian faith could be used to enforce obedience and increase their market value, the slaves had long since established their underground version of the faith. They were building their own "invisible institution" or underground church.[6]

Black Christianity is more than Euro-American Christianity plus a response to racist oppression. Mitchell writes:

> The belief system which had spread naturally across West Africa was characterized by a *positive view* of human experience, the spirit world, and the wise and powerful and good God who created the whole business.[7]

Whites seized upon the superstitious elements of some blacks who had a fear-ridden world view. They concluded that this was typical of all blacks. They assumed that the bizarre was universal for blacks and the only vision of reality available to them. Mitchell correctly points to the manner in which blacks were able to endure hardships which broke the white indentured servants and Indian slaves. For the most part they remained healthy and sane. No other explanation is adequate except that they brought with them from Africa a religious background which prepared them to pass through this adversity.[8] Mitchell observes:

> Blacks were able to take it, not because they were dumb and unaware . . . but because they had a traditional pattern of trusting God and life and adapting their demands to the limits of

reality. Needs which were still unmet, together with final inter-
pretations of human experience, were trusted to the *future* action
of a good God, creator of a benevolent universe.[9]

Gayraud Wilmore has written a definitive study on black
religion and the black church tradition. He argues that black
religion is something more and something less than white
Christianity.[10] Black Christianity, according to Wilmore, has
its origin in Africa. Wilmore observes:

> There was, from the beginning, a fusion between a highly devel-
> oped and pervasive feeling about the hierophantic nature of
> historical experience, flowing from the African religious past,
> and a radical and programmatic secularity, related to the experi-
> ence of slavery and oppression, which constituted the essential
> and most significant characteristic of Black religion. The dialec-
> tical relationship of these two predominant elements of the Black
> religious consciousness was institutionalized in the historic
> Black churches and in the communal and associational group-
> ings which grew up around and have, by no means, severed their
> connection with the churches.[11]

A person who is relatively free to determine his or her
destiny raises different questions from those raised by persons
who are slaves. Blacks have lived through cultural shock and
all manner of oppression at every historical moment. They
have been able to draw upon the resources of their distinctive
religious tradition to interpret the meaning of the black religious experience and to find a saving strength for meeting the
crises. Wilmore observes:

> Blacks have used Christianity, not as it was delivered to them by
> segregated white churches, but as its truth was authenticated to
> them in the experience of suffering, to reinforce an ingrained
> religious temperament and to produce an indigenous religion
> oriented to freedom and human welfare.[12]

Wilmore and Mitchell are in close agreement regarding
the African roots of black religion. The first chapter of Wilmore's book traces the emergence of the slave's religion and
the birth of the black church. Wilmore, more than Mitchell,

stresses the political focus of the religious expression which took shape in the black community. He mentions Islam and voodoo among the slaves, but gives most of his attention to the Christian development among them. Black religion, Wilmore notes, became a religion of an oppressed people. White abolitionism contributed to its militancy, but it was inherently a religion of freedom. Black religion is concerned about the liberation of the whole person—body, mind, and soul. Wilmore believes that this holistic understanding can be traced to Africa.

> The indispensable condition for life and human fulfillment in the religious and philosophical tradition of Africa is freedom—the untrammeled, unconditional freedom to be, to exist, and to express the power of Being fully and creatively for the sheer joy and profound meaning of *Muntu,* man.[13]

Another important drift in Wilmore's discussion is his mention of developments elsewhere among Africans in the New World, e.g., in Haiti and the West Indies.[14] He notes that African survivals are greater among Catholics than among puritan Protestants. Furthermore, colonial societies seem to have produced a class of mixed-bloods as a buffer between blacks and whites. A three-tiered society gave more mobility to slaves than the two-tiered society in the United States.[15] Wilmore nevertheless contends that black religion transmutes spiritual energy into a political movement for freedom. Joseph R. Washington, Jr., provides a convenient summary when he asserts:

> Born in slavery, weaned in segregation and reared in discrimination, the religion of the Negro folk was chosen to bear the roles of both protest and relief.[16]

We have noted from the writers thus far cited an affirmative attitude toward the African roots of black religion. They also hold a positive view of many elements of African traditional religion absorbed into black religion providing a foundation for the establishment of the black church. But this view is not universally held. Eugene D. Genovese represents a different reading of the religion of slaves. His massive studies cannot be ignored. We will briefly but critically examine his point of view.

Genovese reads his sources through Western eyes. He therefore places greater confidence in Euro-American experts on Africa than he does on African or black sources. As a result there are in his discussion many of the perceptions found in almost all "colonial" histories of Africa. He reads both polytheism and deism into West African traditional religion.[17] His view is almost universally rejected by African scholars.[18]

His assertion, in the same place, that West Africans had no sense of sin is also being called into question. J. O. Awolalu of Nigeria has written a definitive essay which provides a convincing refutation of this assumption.[19] Genovese is to be respected for his attempt to trace the African roots of black religion in order to better understand the religion of the slaves, but his sources have misled him. As a result he places too much emphasis upon the immoral, superstitious, and magical aspects of this experience. Some of Genovese's sources are good when he gets into Afro-American history, but his perspectives are marred by a false orientation in the African origins. His book is worth reading, but my preference is for other sources. I do not reject his work because he is of another race, but because the foundation for his conclusions is challenged by overwhelming evidence to the contrary.

What we have to deal with, then, is a religious tradition developed in Africa, transported to the New World by the slaves and transformed by them, through the encounter with the Bible and Christianity, into a unique form of Christianity. Upon this experience and reinterpretation there sprang up the black "invisible" church during slavery and the black institutional church, in force after the emancipation. We turn now to consider the black church as it existed historically in slavery and freedom.[20]

II. THE ORIGIN AND DEVELOPMENT OF THE BLACK CHURCH UNTIL EMANCIPATION

The term "invisible institution," coined by E. Franklin Frazier, portrays the earliest slave initiation into Christianity.[21] It was a sort of underground church for the practice and experience of religion by blacks as slaves. But since Frazier argues that slavery totally uprooted blacks in all forms of social cohesion, he is not our accepted guide.[22] Differences on this matter will lead necessarily to the rereading of the religious tradition. We will continue to insist that there is both continuity and discontinuity between African and Afro-American life which history and circumstance have not blotted out.[23] I can accept Frazier's figure of speech to describe the reality of an underground church during the slavery period. Miles Mark Fisher writes frequently and decisively concerning these "secret meetings" which "instilled the morality of the African cult."[24] Fisher, a church historian and pastor, is an acknowledged authority on the black spirituals. Fisher is interested in the manner in which song and dance related to these religious gatherings of slaves. As a historian, however, he sanctions the carryover of the African influence on black religion.

Frazier argued that slavery caused blacks to lose their African religious heritage—i.e., the religious cults and myths of Africa lost their significance for them. The Christian religion provided a new basis of social solidarity among the slaves, since practically all their African cultural and religious bearings were destroyed. Christianity offered a new orientation toward existence in the alien environment for the bewildered slaves. According to Frazier, blacks embraced the otherworldly tenets of the new religion and accepted the white master's teaching of obedience and fidelity as primary virtues.[25] What Frazier has said is half true. It is not possible to affirm the "radicalism" that Wilmore writes about if one accepts Frazier's premises.[26] If we follow Frazier's reading, the foundations of black theology would be removed. What

this indicates is that there are no value-free sources. All
materials must be read with critical perception and the evidence weighed.

It is true that the Christian religion was used by whites as
a means of social control. James O. Buswell comments on the
use of the Bible in the effort to rationalize slavery.

> The appeal to Scripture has been in the defense of slavery as well
> as the attack upon it. Slavery has had to face Scripture at every
> turn in the form of legal, social, racial and purely doctrinal
> thrusts. This has been true because the fundamental basis of
> slavery is a racial doctrine to which Scripture will always be
> opposed. Yet Scripture was woven into the very fabric of the
> defense of the system of slavery.[27]

White Christians used simple catechisms to attempt to
convince blacks, and perhaps themselves, that slavery had
divine sanction as an institution, and that eternal salvation
was understood as the slave's reward for faithful obedience
and service to the slave master.[28] What we know now is that
the passivity of slaves was often a survival technique. It was
not the way the slaves really understood the Bible or the
Christian religion.

Fisher reminds us that blacks who met together without
authorization were guilty of civil disobedience. South Carolina enacted a law against "all unlawful assemblies" in 1819.
Patrol officers were charged with the responsibility of
upholding the law. These were often poor, landless whites
who were jealous of the slaveholders and held the slaves in
the greatest contempt. Since these poor whites could not
attack the master, they became patrolmen who were determined to take their spite out on the slaves. Worship was
against the law—the slaveholders feared insurrection. A secret place was hard to find with "patter-rollers" all around.
If they were caught worshiping, a brutal death was a possibility. Yet the slaves gathered in worship.[29]

Fisher wrote that spirituals told black slaves what to do

if they discovered that a patrol was on their trail. They should run for their lives. "Run, Nigger, Run" became so popular, we are told, that many white people sang it. It was one of the oldest plantation songs. But the spiritual which began with "jine de band" is perhaps more graphic in its meaning. It also illustrates the bifocal message of the spirituals. Mary ran from an early morning secret meeting in order to escape the consequences of being at an unlawful assembly of slaves. This is easily associated with Biblical Mary at the tomb of Jesus. The two meanings are confused. The slave master would accept the Biblical version, but slaves associated it with flight from an early morning secret meeting. The songs go as follows:

> 1. O run, Mary run,
>   Hallelu, hallelu!
>   O run, Mary run,
>   Hallelujah!
> 2. It was early in de mornin',
>   Hallelu, hallelu!
>   It was early in de mornin',
>   Hallelujah! etc.[30]

The point is made. From the very beginning of their encounter with Christianity blacks associated it with freedom from slavery. They did not abandon their spirituality or their belief in life after death. It was precisely because they valued life for their loved ones that they conquered the fear of death. All black cultists who frequented the secret meetings of slaves were of necessity prepared to accept a violent death.[31]

Fisher has traced the evolution of the religious institutions of blacks through spirituals. Spirituals were devotional songs of the black masses. They chronicle the religious development of blacks, but, at the same time, they describe the conditions under which blacks had to live.

Fisher provides a chart to illustrate the evolution of the religious institutions of blacks:

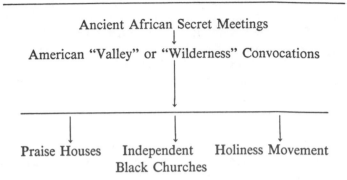

Fisher asserts that the African secret meetings were transplanted to the Americas. These secret meetings of "praise" were institutionalized in the island communities as praise houses and these assemblies gave rise to the independent black churches. The earliest known black church was established at Silver Bluff, South Carolina, in 1773. Later in the eighteenth century the Bethel African Methodist Episcopal Church and the St. Thomas Protestant Episcopal Church sprang up in Philadelphia from the benevolent Free African Society of male members only and dedicated their first houses of worship in 1794. The first organization of the African Methodist Episcopal Zion denomination was instituted in New York City in 1796 in praise services of ten men. The holiness movement was contained, at first, within established churches until 1889, when this tradition was broken.[32]

The theology of this movement among blacks, according to Fisher, was not orthodox—it was the traditional beliefs of the secret meetings. Music consisted of spirituals. African musical instruments were not available. But the rhythm, the feet beating out the time, the syncopation of gospel choruses carry on the African tradition. Preaching was often a singsong affair with deep guttural accompaniment like weeping or moaning, the reading from the Bible was a matter of great importance and shouting was a part of the devotional experience.[33]

According to Fisher, spirituals reflected the social conditions under which blacks were forced to live. Slave society was divided into two classes: the house servants and the field hands. The house servants usually were the best off as far as work, food, and lodging were concerned. The black masses were field hands. These were half fed, poorly housed, ignorant, licentious, and often maimed. They lacked opportunity for improving their lot and they lived a dehumanized existence in abject poverty. But often observers were mystified that even though they were treated so badly they did not appear brokenhearted—they seemed lighthearted. Fisher concludes, "They found much to laugh at when Americans did not even smile."[34]

Du Bois is perhaps also correct when he writes that the slaves sang "sorrow songs," for they were weary at heart. Even so, blacks showed little fear of death, but talked in familiar terms about it. Blacks, according to Du Bois, borrowed from the surrounding culture, but everything seemed to undergo characteristic change when used by the slaves. This was true of Bible phrases. For instance, Du Bois observed, "Weep, O captive daughter of Zion" is turned into "Zion, weep-a-low," and the wheels of Ezekiel are turned in the mystic dreaming of the slave:

> There's a little wheel a-turnin'
> In-a-my heart.

In brief, in spite of this tragic soul life, despair often changed to triumph and calm confidence. Du Bois writes:

> Through all the sorrow of the sorrow songs, there breathes a hope—a faith in the ultimate justice of things. . . . Sometimes it is a faith in life, sometimes a faith in death, sometimes assurance of boundless justice in some fair world beyond. But whichever it is, the meaning is always clear; that sometime,

somewhere, men will judge men by their souls and not by their skins.[35]

James Cone, drawing upon the writings of John Lovell and Miles Mark Fisher, comes to the conclusion we have endorsed here, that the spirituals recite the social as well as the religious history of black people, beginning in Africa. The assumption that spirituals are historical documents supports the view that African music recites the history of a people. When Africans came to the United States they brought the art of storytelling through music. The spirituals reflect the African background of black religion more than any influence from white American Christianity.[36] Cone goes on to assert that the spirituals provide the historical context for understanding the religion and theology of the slaves.[37] With this I am in basic agreement. It follows that such an understanding undergirds the theology and mission of the black church.

Having said that, I do not reject outright the otherworldly, compensatory reading of the spirituals by Benjamin E. Mays.[38] While I do feel an uneasiness about the emphasis Mays has employed in his classic study of black literature as a theologian, I do feel that his reading has some truth in it. My impression would be that both Cone and Mays approach the theological meaning of the spirituals at a sociopolitical level. Cone finds militancy and Mays finds quietism. Howard Thurman, it seems to me, offers an interpretation at a deeper level. It is an intuitive level where the rational and the irrational, the conscious and the unconscious, the social and the psychological meet. Thurman finds the clue to the meaning of the spiritual in the religious consciousness itself. Slaves are determined to *be* in a society which seeks to eliminate their being. They affirm their dignity as persons in spite of any and all adverse circumstances. Stripped to the bare nakedness of their spirits, deprived of the power of their own destiny, the slaves found a way to hold their personhood together.[39] For Thurman, the dignity the slaves sought includes the quest for social justice, the building of community. Mysticism and social change merge in Thurman's perspective.

Howard Thurman represents an aspect of black religion almost overlooked by recent black theologians. It is the deep "spirituality" of the black religious tradition. The spell of either-or logic over many black scholars makes them unable to mediate between various options. Black slaves sensed this tension and reflected it in the spirituals. Black theologians must find a way to blend the rich spirituality of black religious experience with the militant quest for earthly freedom. We desperately need writers who will build upon the legacy of Thurman without losing their passion for social justice. This seems to be a real possibility if we work from within our own tradition. Harold A. Jackson, Jr., has made the attempt with a measure of success. Jackson writes:

> The *modus operandi* of the Spirituals is that of opening up not only levels of reality but also of the soul. It is out of the collective unconsciousness of the slave communities that the peculiar symbolism of the Spirituals come about. . . . Since the Spirituals helped the slave pose the ontological question of being, it was easy for the slave to see that the fierce reality of life was related to the existential situation of life. If freedom was sought for spiritual being, then why could not freedom be sought for physical being? Thus informed by the ontic self, the slave was able to use circumlocution and allegory to disguise acts of assembly and/or escape.[40]

III. A LOOK AT BLACK CHURCH THEOLOGY BEFORE EMANCIPATION

James Cone writes about the pre-Civil War black church. He is mainly concerned about protest. The black church is, in fact, from its inception, the precursor of black power. The black church perceived that freedom and equality are the essence of humanity. Protest and action were the early marks of the black church's uniqueness. Oppression based on race was nationwide. Northern white churchgoers did not regard blacks as equals and therefore regulated the affairs of church

life in their own interest. This is why Richard Allen walked
out of St. George's Methodist Episcopal Church in Philadelphia as early as 1787.[41]

Cone reminds us that the Reverend Henry Highland Garnet advocated outright rebellion. He asserted that the spirit of
liberty is a gift from God, and God endows the slave with the
zeal to break the chains of slavery. The Reverend Nathaniel
Paul was sure that God hated slavery and was actively involved in its elimination.[42] Cone asserts that the black church
is the only church in America which remained recognizably
Christian during pre-Civil War days.[43] But a weakness in
Cone's argument is a lack of appreciation of the African roots
of black religion.[44] Wilmore pushes a similar position, as far as
the "radicalism" of black religion is concerned. He speaks of
Denmark Vesey, Nat Turner, and Henry Highland Garnet as
"generals in the Lord's army."[45] But Wilmore connects the
black tradition with its African roots, as Cone does not.[46]

The orientation in Africa is our past. It is also related to
our present and future as a people, as churches, and as families. This emphasis is lacking in Cone's writings. Because of
the influence of his program at home and abroad, even in
Africa, this omission is regrettable. This purely "political"
reading of black theology neutralizes the impact of black
theology in most of postcolonial Africa. Kwesi A. Dickson
of Ghana has relegated the entire program of black theology
to southern Africa.[47] And Allan Boesak of South Africa, who
has written a definitive study of black theology on both conti-
nents, sees Cone as too regional and without a sound social
critique.[48] Perhaps the most serious lack in Cone is that he
does not anchor black thought and experience in the whole
African/Afro-American tradition.[49] This would provide a
sounder basis for even the political focus he has, to say nothing of the rich cultural and spiritual elements in this material.
From this common historical and cultural base, he could find
a point of contact with all peoples of African descent whether
in Africa or in the New World. Even his fine discussion on
"social existence" has not ventured in this more fruitful di-

rection. Social existence as viewed by Cone is still the Afro-American past which does not define black experience.[50] Such a shift in Cone's thought would, however, modify the presuppositions of his entire program—e.g., his exclusive christocentrism, his "oppression-liberation" formula, and his dialectical way of thinking which is, in fact, pro-Western (Greek-Teutonic).

Cecil Cone has accepted the fact of African survivals. He goes so far as to say that Africans "were not converted to Christianity but they converted Christianity to themselves."[51] His research on black religious experience is extensive. What he comes up with is a view of God as "the Almighty Sovereign God." This is for Cecil Cone an "Africanized God." The proper response to such a God is submission and celebration. He mentions with approval the work of Bishop Henry McNeal Turner, and even Martin Luther King, who attacked racist oppression with this understanding of God.[52] His main focus, however, seems to be on the "celebrative" aspects of black religion among the slaves as they worshiped this God. Cecil Cone writes:

> The only appropriate foundation for black theology is black religion. Forged from African religion and Biblical Christianity in the crucible of American slavery, it focuses upon the encounter with the Almighty Sovereign God and issues in conversion. It has been expressed in a continuous tradition of celebration and struggle from slave days to the present time.[53]

Cecil Cone's perspectives are in the right direction as far as the African/Afro-American connection is concerned. But I am not satisfied with the doctrine of God he forges out of this continuous religious tradition. God's power should always be seen in relation to other attributes such as love and justice. Otherwise, God can inspire dread as well as devotion. Furthermore, God's sovereignty can demote as well as promote human dignity. Celebration by individuals over their conversion can bring inner peace, even inner strength, but it can also foster an irrelevant otherworldliness. Of course Cecil is only stating his position in order to criticize James Cone, Joseph Washington, and myself for embracing "black power" as a theological motif. While his critique is valuable, he needs now to show the way forward.

Changing cultural, political, and economic factors affect theology and religious practice. The Mormon attitude toward slavery before emancipation is a case in point. The Mormon race policy has brought slavery theology into our time. The recent "revelation" to the head of this religious movement, that black males may be admitted to the priesthood, should be examined in this light. Racism was codified by the Mormons after they moved into Missouri. There they encountered the slavocracy and allowed the social situation to determine their theology. Slavery and not God provided the "revelation" that sanctioned racism in the Mormon Church for more than a hundred years. This is dramatized by the fact that prior to the Mormons' settlement in Missouri, they had been active in the abolitionist movement.[54] The Mormons were even challenged by the old settlers for being too lenient toward the blacks. They were in ideological and economic conflict with the local white population over slavery. When *The Book of Mormon* was published in 1830, Joseph Smith indicated that God made no distinction based on race (II Nephi 26:33).[55] Smith even prophesied a slave insurrection.[56] Mormons were inviting free blacks to Missouri and admitting them to the church. But they were openly opposed by the old settlers in July, 1833.[57] The Mormons were actually evicted from Jackson County, Missouri, for their opposition to slavery. The policy of excluding blacks from the priesthood emerged about 1834 in response to social, political, and economic sanctions against the Mormons.[58] This policy was set forth in *The Book of Doctrine and Covenants* in 1835.[59]

The Mormon case is a clear example of how social and economic factors influence religion and theology. It is, therefore, not surprising that the theological climate of the slavery period is so differently perceived by different authors. Here

I will present two brief examples of one-sided interpretatic of the formation of the slave's religious beliefs. In 192 W. R. Wilson wrote an essay on the black slave's attitud toward life and death in which he said:

> My thesis is that the religion of Africa disappeared from the consciousness of the American slave; that the slave himself by contact with a new environment, became a decidedly different person, having a new religion, a primitive Christianity, with central emphasis, not upon this world, but upon heaven.[60]

It is Wilson's view that Africans had no positive view of the afterlife.

> The men of Africa knew no land of sunshine beyond the . . . grave; but the American slave . . . did not inherit the fears of Africa.[61]

Wilson sets out to prove that slaves came culturally and religiously empty to be filled with American Christianity. He argues that the black slave found in America a "Christian atmosphere."[62] Christianity brought to the slave words of hope and salvation, a message of companionship with the heavenly father.[63] Wilson reads the spirituals with a completely otherworldly frame of reference.[64] What Wilson presents as the slaves' religion is not all false, but it is not the total picture either. His discussion is based upon misinformation and limited information; therefore his conclusions are misleading.

Another example similar in nature is Newbell N. Puckett's 1931 essay on religious folk beliefs of whites and blacks. Puckett argues that blacks received their religious folk beliefs from whites. The spirituals came from white music.[65] The Protestant religious creed was the same for both races. Even the "wealth of imagery" in black music and black speech came from whites.[66] He is not so sure, however, if blacks received their propensity toward immoral living from whites.[67] Their emotionalism in religious worship came from the white camp meetings.[68] This was true also of their seeing visions.[69] Superstitions among the blacks had a European origin. The Sea Island "shout" is harder for Puckett to explain. This was a formal, well-organized group dance among blacks. It was the same in religious worship as in secular festivities.[70]

Puckett concludes that "it is the backward folk who tend most strongly to imitate the more advanced and not to the contrary."[71] He clearly assumes that nothing worth considering can be traced to Africa. This appears to be a value judgment on his part. He does not seem to be concerned about whether anything from the African past survived the slavery experience. He concludes: "The broad creed, or religious belief, of Negroes follows after that of the whites."[72]

The evidence leads us to precisely the opposite conclusion. We have seen in the black church tradition thus far obvious African roots. These roots have borne fruit in the experience of Afro-Americans in their religious life. The experience of slavery caused the black encounter with the Bible and Christianity to take a distinctive direction. The understanding of religion and church propagated by white teachers, who themselves lived in a contradiction to their own creed, was not the version of the Christian faith appropriated by black slaves. They somehow blended their African religious consciousness, the experience of oppression, and the Christian gospel into a dynamic mix that deepened their spiritual awareness and their political consciousness at the same time. The African religious consciousness which is holistic—embracing the whole person and all of life, all communal relationships—has triumphed in black Christianity.

CHAPTER IV

Black Church and Family: Reconstruction I to Reconstruction II

Rebellion and protest as well as refuge and support have existed side by side throughout the history of the black church in this country. This was true in the slave states as well as "north of slavery."[1] A one-sided view does not tell the whole story. It is essential, however, to put everything in historical context. The black religious experience has always been a "stride toward freedom." Blacks have had to adapt their programs to meet their freedom needs as circumstances have been altered by pressures from white oppressors. Our minds have been "stayed on freedom," but the means to obtain freedom will vary. At one time the approach may be legal, at another time political, and again it could be economic. It is remarkable how black religious leaders, both clerical and lay, have been able to read the "signs of the times" and act through appropriate means. Black families and churches have been the main institutions participating in the freedom struggle. They have likewise been affected by the social history of black people.

I. FROM INVISIBILITY TO VISIBILITY: THE BLACK CHURCH

Slavery dealt a cruel blow to church and family, the two primary institutions in the black community. It is not possi-

ble to understand the present plight of blacks without return-
ing again and again to slavery. Black leaders insist upon
reviewing this tragic history not because they are sadists, but
because it is not possible to provide a remedy to racism
without considering its cause. The historical roots of racism
in the United States are in slavery. However painful it may
be to look at that inhuman system, we Americans must review that history.

Even the founding fathers of the nation ignored black
equality. Some were slaveholders and their assertion that "all
men are created equal" did not include black slaves. Black
women were exploited from the beginning by white men.
Any cohabitation between black men and white women was
strictly forbidden under threat of death for the black man. It
was immediately written into law that the status of the child
born of interracial unions would be that of the mother. This
meant that since white men had their way with black women,
they could in fact reproduce their own slaves, giving them a
crucial economic advantage.

Judge A. Leon Higginbotham, Jr., writes:

> It was . . . significant from an economic standpoint whether a
> child derived its status from its mother or father. Once it was
> established that a black woman's child took the mother's status,
> the master class gained a crucial economic advantage—its labor
> force reproduced itself. If the legislature had followed the En-
> glish legal doctrine that the status of the child was determined
> by the status of the father, the thousands of Blacks or mulattoes
> whose fathers were white would have been free.[2]

It is clear that the sexual union of white men with black
women was based upon lust. It seems devoid of not only love
but any semblance of humanity even toward the offspring.
What man who has human love for a woman or a child borne
by a woman with whom he has had sexual relations would
subject that child to slavery? We are aware through the
statement by Judge Higginbotham how the law was changed
in order to foster the slave system. Finally, we see the de-

structive impact of the entire scheme upon the black family.

I am extremely suspicious of any studies, however learned, which assert that slavery was not so bad after all and black families were not severely crippled by that inhuman system.[3] A good confession would be the best thing for the soul of America.

We are concerned with presenting a constructive theological statement on the black church as an extended family. The theological arguments about slavery *pro* and *con* are of value as we move forward. Since both sides appealed to the Bible as the main authority, one is moved by the unusual manner in which texts are quoted freely out of context to prove a point.

In 1857, George Armstrong argued that neither Christ nor his apostles regarded slavery as a sin. The apostles received slaveholders into the church without raising any issues regarding their slaveholding. Paul sent back a fugitive slave to his own master again, asserting the master's right to the service of the slave. Finally, the apostles enjoined the relative duties of master and slave. They were concerned only with Christian duties and motives which have nothing to do with slavery.[4]

Armstrong's case rested upon two basic arguments. First, he was concerned with hermeneutics. He accepted the Bible as the sole authority for the life of the church. He seemed to argue primarily from the New Testament, but he was concerned broadly with "law and testimonies." Second, he raised the issue of the "jurisdiction" of church and state. Armstrong concluded that the church has jurisdiction in regard to the spiritual nature of man and the future life. The state, on the other hand, has jurisdiction over the present life. It follows that the church has no jurisdiction over the institution of slavery or its removal. While there is an indirect relation between church and state, the person being both Christian and citizen, the direct jurisdiction over slavery belongs to the state. The role of the church is personal, private, spiritual. Armstrong wrote:

> In the case of a race of men in slavery, the work which God has appointed his church . . . is to labor to secure in them a Christian life on earth and meekness for his heavenly kingdom.[5]

This book, written in support of slavery, is representative.[6] We also have arguments against slavery by abolitionist theologians. In most cases these seem to be counterarguments against slavery theologians. The abolitionist theologians were quite perceptive at certain points. They did not agree as to whether servitude among the Jews was really slavery. They were certain, however, that the Egyptian bondage of the Jews was slavery. They also drew an analogy between the slavery the Jews experienced in Egypt and black slavery in the United States.[7] The abolitionists had great difficulty when they took up the New Testament because of the "silence" of Jesus and the conservatism of Paul. They could mainly argue that the New Testament "offered no justification for slavery."[8] Abolitionists used the Bible to condemn Southerners for their sins of commission and Northerners for their sin of omission on the slavery issue. While the abolitionist theologians were questionable in their manner of appeal to Scripture, their arguments resonate with a deep sense of humanity. Shanks writes:

> What the abolitionists were trying to do was to justify a profound moral sentiment by the highest authority they knew, and through all their arguments we must recognize this ethical element—a grasping after that righteousness which exalteth a nation, a longing to rid their country of sin which is a reproach to any people.[9]

What we have discussed above is what white theologians were saying about black slavery. This cannot be the last word; for blacks, the victims of this inhuman system, made their own contribution to this discussion. It was they who suffered, and their reflection has the weight of the authority of experience. James Cone, seeking the connection between thought and social existence, argues that the meaning of the creed for members of the African Methodist Episcopal

Church differs from that for white Methodists. The motto of the black denomination is: "God Our Father, Christ Our Redeemer, Man Our Brother." Cone reasons that the origin of this black church and the grounds for its continued separation indicate a different theology.

> Since Richard Allen and Daniel Payne did not act the same way as their white contemporaries, I must conclude that they invested the words "God," "Christ," and "brotherhood" with different meaning from those of the white preachers of the Methodist Church.[10]

Richard Allen understood God as the ground of freedom and the source of black people's affirmation of personhood. Daniel Payne, according to Cone, understood the theodicy question not from Augustine and Hume, but from the Bible in relation to black people's experience of "God at prayer meeting on Sunday night and of the slave driven in the field on Monday morning."[11] Black slaves understood Christ also as they read the Bible in the light of their slavery. Jesus was a source of courage and power in black life to struggle against injustice and oppression.[12] Henry M. Turner, Cone writes, sees the connection between his humanity and God's fatherhood.[13] Cone urges ministers, bishops, and lay persons in the A.M.E. Church to forsake the white version of Christianity and reclaim the faith of Allen, Payne, and Turner. The name of the church, Cone writes, "reflected the members of a church who believed that God is the father of all, that Christ is the redeemer of all, and that all peoples are brothers and sisters in the faith."[14] This church was founded for the liberation of poor black people. Richard Allen and Daniel Payne, we are told, represent "the liberating force of God's presence among black people."[15]

This essay by Cone puts in historical perspective the understanding of theology and church in one of the strongest black denominations. Cone's renunciation of the classical theological tradition may be counterproductive. This is especially true since some of the giants among the theologians of the early church hailed from Africa. It would be useful to know even more about their contribution. But on the whole, the drift of his observations are useful as we learn to appreciate the thought and action of black religious leaders and thinkers during the last century. Charles H. Nichols reminds us that the ex-slave narrators saw the judgment of God and God's overriding providence even in the death of a cruel master. He writes:

> The Methodist and Baptist sects appealed to the slaves because they "preached deliverance to the captives." And in their own secret religious meetings they took comfort from the often repeated Biblical stories which answered to their condition: Daniel in the lions' den, the children of Israel enslaved by Pharaoh, Christ crucified by the influential people about him.[16]

Nichols does not neglect to mention the impact of the "emotional religious observances" of slaves. But he insists that most slaves did not accept the dogma that God had made them slaves. Most slaves felt that the moral universe was on the side of their freedom. "Even the more conciliatory slaves frequently looked for judgment day when the despots who ruled over them would get their just deserts."[17]

II. HISTORICAL PERIODS AND THEIR IMPACT ON THE BLACK CHURCH

Ruby F. Johnson, in her study *The Development of Negro Religion,* notes three stages or periods of black religion, based primarily upon the shifts in its emotional tone.[18] The first, the "inceptional" stage, extended from the beginning of black religion in America to the Civil War. It was marked by supernaturalism, simple rudiments of Christianity, and emotionalism. The second stage was noted for the rise of race consciousness and efforts by black leaders to secure freedom of worship and freedom to be persons. But this stage was likewise predominantly otherworldly—its emphasis and objectives were directed toward heaven. This "developmental" stage began with emancipation and ended about 1914. Johnson observes that there was steady growth with a focus on civil and social rights. When compared with the earlier stage, there was more active participation in government and social life during this latter period. Heavenly elements were still central in black religion, but somewhat diminished. The third stage, that of "transition," began in 1914 and continued to 1945 when the book was published. There was tension in this period, which saw both a decline of emotionalism in black religion and a desire to return to it. There was a wane in religious zeal and a transference of attention to issues in this world. Churches were more involved in political activities, social life, and recreation as well as concern for the total national scene.

Essentially I agree with Olin Moyd's critique of Johnson's typology. Moyd writes:

> It was the third stage of the development of Negro religion which comprised the main portion of her study and throughout she was preoccupied with the degree and shifts of emotionalism in black religion. This approach is helpful in tracing the shift in emotional expressions in black religion, but it is totally inadequate for an understanding of the theology which undergirded any and all black religious expressions.[19]

It is obvious that Johnson's reading of black religious experience is problematic. Her yardstick for measurement is essentially emotional. She associates heightened emotionalism with otherworldliness and she reasons in either-or fashion—either emotionalism or activism. Her perspective is brought ready-made to the examination of black religion. Her presuppositions do not emerge out of a phenomenological encounter with black religious experience itself. If she were examining white religious experience, much of her evaluation would ring true. Black religious experience is different, however. Radicalism and deep piety (often intensely emotional) often coexist. She misses the "rebellion" in slave religion and she concludes that the black church has only

been socially active as it experienced an emotional decline.
She did not move forward into the Martin Luther King era,
but King built upon a tradition already established. King's
ministry dramatically demolishes her thesis. It was centered
in traditional black worship and fellowship, but this fervor
fueled the flames of a robust activism.

The reassessment of the historical periods of black religion
will serve toward a better understanding of the two primary
institutions under investigation here—the black church and
the black family. Olin Moyd has come up with helpful guide-
lines. He is mainly concerned with the development of black
religion from the emancipation to the present. Moyd's interest, like that of the present writer, is essentially theological.
History is a necessary aid to theological reflection. We had
a great deal to say about the development of black religion
up until the Civil War. Therefore, we are presently preoccupied with the development from that period to the present.

Moyd divides this period into five convenient subperiods:
(1) the Formative period, from the Civil War through Reconstruction; (2) the Maturation period, from Reconstruction to
the beginning of the Great Migration (1914); (3) the Expansion-Renaissance period, from the Great Migration to the
beginning of World War II; (4) the Passive Protest period,
from World War II to 1955; and (5) the Radical Reassertion
period, from 1955 to the present.[20]

The Formative period was a time of unparalleled growth
for black churches and denominations. During the Reconstruction era, black churches led the black community in
political involvement. This period resembled the Black
Power era of the late 1960's. During Reconstruction, blacks
served in the Congress of the United States. They served as
school superintendents, postmasters, state treasurers, state
secretaries, and lieutenant governors. Black churches were
bases of operation for social, educational, and political action. Churches were also places for repose, for spiritual comfort. During this period black churches developed a deepened
understanding of the Christian faith. Black theology was not

so much committed to writing, but it radiated throughout the oral tradition of this period.

The Maturation period followed Reconstruction, according to Moyd. Through a "compromise" between North and South in 1876, blacks received the most drastic setback in their history. Virtually all the gains of the Reconstruction period were wiped out. Moyd notes:

> Blacks were used as a political football. After the election of Hayes the state legislatures in every state of the Union passed laws stripping Blacks of rights they had gained during the era of Reconstruction; Civil Rights Acts were struck down by the Supreme Court. Jim Crow laws went into effect in many states. Federal troops were withdrawn from the South. The Freedmen's Bureau became less and less effective. There was a loss of white missionary zeal and effectiveness. Black politicians were virtually weeded out through various and devious means . . . and measures were taken to make sure that none got elected again. . . . Disfranchisement was effectuated through such measures as poll taxes, literary tests, previous voting records, grandfather clauses, and knowledge of the Constitution. . . . In 1896 . . . the Supreme Court came out with its separate but equal decree which set a pattern of legal separation of the races for the next century.[21]

During this period the black church held its own. It became more mature. It was busy refining its theology and ministry to meet the needs of black people. Total separation of blacks and whites took place, especially in the South. Segregation in the church was more complete now than during slavery. Black churches had established their independence and power. Leadership had been developed and a deeper knowledge of the freedom of the gospel was present. By 1890 there were nearly twenty-four thousand black churches in the country with a total membership of two and a half million. Nationwide, ten blacks out of twenty-eight were church members. In the South, one of every two was a church member. Even blacks who were not church members attended black churches and took part in their activities.

There was an organized black church for every sixty black
families in the United States. Many blacks were Baptists and
the Methodists also claimed many.

Moyd writes:

> It is clear that the black church reached full autonomy. It was
> virtually, totally separated from the white churches. It sur-
> rounded and shaped every era of black life. During this period
> the black church reached its theological maturation. And any-
> thing which happened in the black church's theological under-
> standing of redemption since its era of maturation is only a
> matter of shifts in emphasis.[22]

By way of summary, Moyd argues that by the end of the
Maturation period (1914) segregated Sabbaths were established and black denominations were autonomous. They had
fully developed styles of worship tempered with African survivals. Adaptations and reinterpretations of doctrines and
Scriptures by blacks were developed. And finally, songs,
prayers, testimonies, and the orientations behind the sermons
became normative for the future. Moyd concludes that religious thought and expression developed among blacks during
the Formative and the Maturation periods were carried to
the North by blacks during the Great Migration.[23]

The black church moved *en masse* from plantation to
ghetto during the Great Migration. Moyd designates this as
the Expansion-Renaissance period. This period came to a
close with World War II. During this period blacks were
pushed out of the South by the force of white hostility and
inhumanity.[24] By 1914 boll weevils and floods had diminished
the crops, making black survival in the South most difficult.
Blacks were attracted to the North by the rise of northern
industries. World War I was in progress, giving rise to even
more industrialization. Blacks were lured to the North in
search of better economic, housing, and social conditions.

During and shortly after World War I, nearly a half million blacks left the South. They clustered in such places as
Chicago, Cleveland, and New York City. Like many similar

experiences in black history, this move was conceived by devout blacks as a divine event. But if the Great Migration was conceived as an exodus, Harlem—for example—was not the Promised Land. Moyd writes:

> It is evident that Blacks saw the whole movement as redemption in process. They could easily compare what was happening to them with the exodus of the Hebrews. So, it was the hand of the Almighty God guiding them through the exodus experience. However, unlike the Hebrews in the Moses story, upon arriving in the Promised Land—the North—it was not so promising after all. . . . In the North Blacks found themselves under the domination of new Pharaohs. They found themselves crammed into ghettos with very limited opportunities to earn a surviving wage.[25]

The established black churches of the North could not absorb the flood of newcomers. Black Baptist and Methodist churches experienced astounding growth and yet there was a lack of space to accommodate all the newcomers. Furthermore, the established black churches of the North were often too ritualistic and formal in worship style to appeal to this mass of black southern folk. The newcomers gave rise to black sects and cults and the storefront churches. The Father Divine and Daddy Grace movements developed to fill this void. We could also mention the rise of Marcus Garvey, the Nation of Islam, and the Black Jews as representative of the religious ferment among blacks in the North. For the most part, however, these new groups, some Baptist and most Pentecostal churches, carried on the religious traditions from the South.

Moyd notes a relationship between this religious expansion and the emergence of the "Harlem Renaissance" in literature and the fine arts. The Renaissance was an expression of the discontent of black people with the experience of oppression in the North. Dialect was denounced by the writers in the movement. They sought to use the best English in order to overcome the stereotypes imposed upon black literature by white writers. They did not perceive that their efforts would be fruitless in overcoming the distorted image of blacks in the white mind. What this black Renaissance did accomplish, however, was to give rise to black culture and pride. Moyd's conclusion is, I believe, sound:

> While the activities of the Blacks during the Renaissance were done largely outside the church, the views of the writers and participants were molded in or by the black church and the course they traveled was mapped in the black church.[26]

We note a decline in this renaissance of artistic and literary expression during the depression years of the 1930's. This creative impulse within the black community, as we now know, was not to be realized again until the middle 1960's. The black community at this point in history participated in what Moyd describes as a "passive protest" period which concerns us now.

The period of Passive Protest ran from World War II until 1955. The degree of black church leadership varied according to the social and economic conditions of each period. It was related to the degree of hostility and oppression blacks had to endure. In the late 1920's and into the 1930's, blacks faced the blunt edge of a national depression while having to absorb the intense hostility of whites (both native and foreign born, Northern as well as Southern) who themselves were being afflicted by the depression. Black suffering increased and the black church, the only institution controlled by blacks, was forced to turn its main efforts toward the survival of black people. For instance, black churches were used as distribution centers for government food. Black churches were not in a position to move forward forcefully on the liberation front when people were facing mass starvation. It is Moyd's thesis that blacks have known how to survive by shifting to passive protest when active protest would lead only to mass suicide.[27]

In the early stages of World War II the defense industries refused to hire an appreciable number of blacks or to upgrade the few already employed. A. Philip Randolph, president of the Brotherhood of Sleeping Car Porters, led in organizing for a march on Washington. Randolph, together with key black leaders, was called to Washington for a meeting with President Roosevelt. The nation would have been embarrassed to have this massive black protest in wartime; therefore, there was a willingness to work out a compromise with black leaders. The result of the Randolph-Roosevelt conference was Executive Order 8802, acceptable to black leaders, designed to overcome unfair employment practices based upon race. But this was a wartime edict—its effects were meager and temporary. It is important to note the value of the "black pulpit" in support of this protest. The power of the black press was also manifest.[28] The role of black religion in seeking black liberation is appropriately summarized by Joseph Washington when he writes:

> Born in slavery, weaned in segregation and reared in discrimination, the religion of the Negro folk was chosen to bear roles of both protest and relief. Thus, the uniqueness of black religion is the racial bond which seeks to risk its life for the elusive but ultimate goal of freedom and equality by means of protest and action.[29]

If we do not learn from our history, we are doomed to repeat it. Whites have always been able to control the degree of black protest or to blunt its effectiveness. During the black literary protest, whites won control of that movement by ownership of printing presses and by selective buying of books. For example, Jean Toomer's *Cane* sold only five hundred copies in 1923, the first year of its publication.

During the Korean war, blacks believed that they could win economic security, and that this upward socioeconomic mobility would change white attitudes toward them. The black leaders of the Harlem Renaissance, we recall, thought they could do the same by dropping black dialect and using perfect English. Both efforts failed.

The efforts to gain economic parity and social equality

based upon it resulted in two things: (1) Very few blacks were able to make their way through the pressures of white power to a real bourgeois status. Many lived, however, in a make-believe world, as if they had achieved such a status. (2) All blacks, of whatever economic status, soon discovered that, in racist America, each one was still a "Negro" or a "Colored Person" or a "Nigger," depending upon who was making the reference. This meant that a black person was not *equal* in personhood to a white person.[30] The need for black liberation was soon to be apparent. Hence protest was to continue in a different form.

The final period discussed by Moyd is the period of Radical Reassertion which dates from 1955 to the present. In my judgment the dates should be from 1954 until about 1966, at which time a different approach was initiated. At the present we will present Moyd's argument and make our amendment later.

Perhaps the most dramatic effort of the black churches to win black freedom began in 1955 when, on December 1, Rosa Parks was arrested for taking a seat reserved for whites on a bus in Montgomery, Alabama. Under the leadership of the Reverend Dr. Martin Luther King, Jr., black churches led a successful boycott. The Southern Christian Leadership Conference (SCLC) was born. This was largely a black church movement with all major civil rights groups lending support. Black churches provided money, staff, demonstrators, meeting space, food, and lodging for this civil rights movement. Moyd writes:

> The civil rights workers from every walk of life borrowed the songs of the black church to drive away the evils of humiliation and the burdens of exhortation. The theme song, "We Shall Overcome" had been lifting the broken spirits of blacks long before the coming of the Civil Rights Movement. It is the theme song about black redemption. The "pray-ins" originated not with the Civil Rights Movement, but with Richard Allen back in 1786. That pray-in was the genesis out of which the African Methodist Episcopal Church evolved.[31]

The present writer would opt for at least four distinct periods from 1954 to the present. While black churches have always responded to the "stride toward freedom" of black people, the pace has accelerated. A close-up look at this general span of time is called for. The first, from 1954 to 1965, we may call the Civil Rights/Integration period. The second, from 1966 to 1972, was the Black Consciousness/ Black Power period. The third, the Reformist period, began in 1973 and ended roughly in 1977. The fourth, the present period, is one of Political Response to Neo-Racism. While this quarter century or more beginning with 1954 has some continuity, it is obvious that it is advantageous to break down this time span into manageable segments for clarification as well as appropriate response and action.

The Supreme Court decision on school desegregation in 1954 created the climate of reflection and action for this entire span of black history. Other legal decisions, executive orders, etc., as well as Dr. King's efforts, were launched in the climate set by the 1954 decision. Having said this, we would not by any means deny the unusual impact of black churches in the liberation push which followed.

It is not necessary to recall the importance of black churches and black theology in the black consciousness/empowerment movement. This is well known and well attested through thought and involvement in the black liberation movement.

Few black leaders caught up in the black church liberation movement in the late 1960's seemed aware that by the early 1970's the peak of that movement had passed. We were moving into a "reformist" phase of the black struggle. Most of the leading black militants were dead, exiled, or in prison. Those who were not "political prisoners" were co-opted by the white system. If there were activists at all, they were now wearing three-piece suits and were asking other blacks to accept middle-class white values and standards. For a historical precedent, we would have to hark back to Booker T. Washington's economic program of racial uplift and the Pu-

ritan ethic. Instead of revolution, we were now seeking reform of the system. We desired to enter the system, through
affirmative action programs. We sincerely believed that this
"bootstrap" approach would enable us to upgrade our status
and that the system would accept us and become more humane. Jesse Jackson's PUSH program is a dramatic example.

Any faith we may have had in the success of this outlook
was being carefully washed away by the rise of a new form
of racism. We had said that we were a distinct people. We
were classified as just another ethnic group. We were merged
into a medley of other ethnic groups, mainly a host of hy-
phenated Americans. We were asked to forget slavery, segregation, discrimination—in fact, four hundred years of mis-
treatment based upon race—and just take our chances with
everybody else.

We were not told that race more than class was the problem.[32] We were not to consider the need for "reparations" for
all the damage that racism has done to every generation of
blacks since 1619.[33] The Supreme Court decision in the
Bakke case should have been the jolt to make blacks aware
that again we have been outfoxed by whites. In this period
when we need a political response to neo-racism, we face the
most difficult test in our assault against racism in our history
in this country. This neo-racism is nationwide. The initiative
came from California and not from Mississippi. Its effects are
most devastating among the black masses and especially the
young. It has a potential for destroying all black institutions,
especially families and churches.

III. HISTORICAL PERIODS AND THEIR IMPACT ON THE BLACK FAMILY

Since the experience of black people for more than a century has been outlined in this chapter, the black family can be
seen in that context. References to the experiences of the black
church may be duplicated in the case of the black family.
This means that this part of our discussion can be brief.

As a result of extensive research on the black family, Eugene D. Genovese concludes that many black men lived up to their responsibility. He states that "probably a majority overcame all obstacles and provided a positive male image for their wives and children."[34] He therefore suggests that we take a fresh look at this situation, for this has much to say about a viable family life. It was true, he observes, that slave men could not protect their women against the insults and abuses of overseers. Slave women understood the plight of black men, who did not lose their masculinity as far as black women were concerned. The women did not expect their men to be killed in a fruitless attempt to demonstrate their masculinity in a paternalistic system. They were not able to function as white men did in political and economic roles, but male-female relations were not at the center of these concerns —it was racism which shut them off. Genovese writes:

> Many men and women resisted the "infantilization," "emasculation," and "dehumanization" inherent in the system's aggression against the slave family. How many? No one will ever know. At issue is the quality of human relationships, which cannot be measured. But there exists as much evidence of resistance and of struggle for a decent family life as of demoralization. A brutal social system broke the spirit of many and rendered others less responsible than human beings ought to be. But enough men came out of this test of fire whole, if necessarily scarred, to demonstrate that slaves had powerful inner resources. A terrible system of human oppression took a heavy toll of its victims, but their collective accomplishment in resisting the system constitutes a heroic story. That resistance provided black people with solid norms for family life and role differentiation, even if circumstances caused a dangerously high lapse from those norms. The slaves from their own experience had come to value a two-parent, male-centered household, no matter how much difficulty they had in realizing the ideal.[35]

I have quoted this argument of Genovese extensively since E. Franklin Frazier, a black sociologist, stressed to the breaking point the black matriarchate thesis. According to Frazier, the black matriarchate was only broken after the Civil War when men won rights of a political and economic sort. Furthermore, the rise of the black church gave black men a new status. Frazier writes:

> The church was under the domination of men, and whatever control it attempted to exercise tended to confirm the man's interest and authority in the family. They found sanction for male ascendancy in the Bible, which, for the newly emancipated slaves, was the highest authority in such matters.[36]

Another way for a man to regain his dominant role within the family, even during slavery, was to purchase his freedom and that of his wife and children. This was a way open only to the most ambitious male slaves. Because of difficult laws governing property rights this was a most complicated route to follow. And yet many black men were able to do this.[37]

The drift of Frazier's discussion is that the black family was the "house of the mother," especially during slavery. In some four chapters he describes the "broken bonds," "unfettered motherhood," "the matriarchate," and "Granny." The argument clearly establishes the thesis that the black family in slavery and beyond was a matriarchy. It is not surprising that the recent controversial Moynihan Report on the black family rested a great deal of its case on Frazier's argument.

There is, no doubt, some truth in this stress on the matriarchate. Frazier is a careful scholar. One has to examine his study seriously, for it is well supported by rigorous research. In an essay by Jessie W. Parkhurst of Tuskegee Institute, a convincing study is presented which lends support to Frazier's thesis. This latter study is concerned with the "Mammy" in the plantation household. The Mammy, usually a black woman of mature years, was the most influential woman on the plantation. She was often more powerful than the master's wife. She directed the household. She counseled the master and his sons, cared for the white children, supervised the servants, both male and female. She was the dominant person among the slaves—even the male members of her family received favors only through her. The affection between the black Mammy and the master's household was broken only by the Civil War. Many of these slave women comforted the white mistress while her sons and husband fought the Civil War to keep the slave woman and her own children in bondage. Some of the slave women showed more love for the master's children than for their own. Some young children responded with such affection that they accepted her as their real mother. Even the most distinguished persons of the old aristocracy of the South boast that they were reared by such a "black Mammy."[38]

Some years ago as a graduate student I discovered that a close white friend of mine befriended me primarily because he was reared by a black woman. He was not from the South. He was from the Northeast. His father was a businessman whose wife had died young and left him with a son and a daughter. One wonders about the internal relations in a black family when for economic reasons a black woman uses up all of her energy and affection in a white household. Much of this history has a contemporary application.

Imposing as the evidence is on the side of a black matriarchate, I fear that if we go all the way down this path, we will see only one side of the picture. A more balanced view needs to be presented. To a great extent the "strengths of black families" studies in opposition to the Moynihan Report have served that end. Again Genovese's insights are helpful. He describes the black male-female relation after emancipation. He notes that black women were strong, even militant, but they backed black men and urged them to enter the political process and support their families. He feels that this transition was possible in black families because there was already greater equality between men and women among blacks. Black women used their enormous strength to support black men. Black men needed assurance to survive, and only the black woman could provide that assurance.[39] This discussion is as relevant as today's news.

Herbert G. Gutman, in *The Black Family in Slavery and*

Freedom, has challenged much previous scholarship on the black family. He has done much of the final demolition work on the Moynihan thesis. But the main purpose of his study is not to determine social policy. It is rather a careful study of black social history with the family as the main point of reference. Gutman studied black families in Buffalo, New York, between 1850 and 1920. He found that 82 to 92 percent of the black families studied were headed by two parents. This led him to undertake the monumental study of *The Black Family.* Later he studied records of at least 10,000 slaves. This was supplemented by case studies on black families on major plantations in North Carolina, South Carolina, and Virginia. His problem was not, What did slavery do to black people? It was, rather, What did blacks do as slaves? He argues that slave behavior and culture were not predetermined by the kind of treatment the slaves received from whites.

Gutman asserts that slaves developed their own cultural patterns, often without dependence on their masters. Slave parents named their children for forebears. This indicates their awareness of blood lines and kinship. Slaves wrote agonizing letters inquiring about family members and kin left behind when they were sold from upper to lower South. This indicates strong family consciousness. Slave women frequently bore children for one or more fathers, but then often settled down to long marriages and demonstrated unusual fidelity.

In his zeal to correct historiographic error, Gutman has not been completely fair to Genovese's *Roll, Jordan, Roll.* Genovese is seen as one who believes black culture was mainly a response to the conditions of the slave system. While we have a more affirmative view of Genovese's study, we can appreciate Gutman's intention. His debate with *Time on the Cross* by Stanley Engerman and Robert Fogel is much more decisive and important. Using an impressive barrage of statistics, these authors argued that if slavery was profitable it must have been at least minimally benign. In a word, you would not abuse humans who were your means to economic betterment. Gutman sees these authors as playing a kind of numbers game and indulging in a type of science fiction which had no resemblance to the actual slave economy. They seem to have no awareness of the devastating effects which slavery had upon human dignity or the measure of suffering it inflicted upon blacks in all their relationships.

Gutman's study provides a wealth of information concerning the black family until 1925. He leaves important questions to be answered. What can we learn from black families that will help us to understand the family bond itself? In what ways are the ties of kinship the ultimate defense against tyranny? Without these ties, black families would have been ultimately demoralized. What was it about the kinship bond that helped people resist the total collapse of families? Through Gutman's study we see that it is difficult to overpower another's will if that will is determined. We observe that commitment to one's kin is, even under the most adverse circumstances, the essence of asserting one's real freedom. This offsets the present attitude which reflects the belief that the family itself is a form of slavery. It rather demonstrates that a profound commitment to one's family may be a real experience of personal freedom. From the study of the black family tradition of black slaves, post-Civil War black sharecroppers, and modern urban black workers we learn a remarkable lesson: the capacity to commit oneself to another enlarges and enriches one's life. It was the willingness to be "tied down" which led black slaves to search for lost loved ones and to invent kinship relations with neighbors when no natural blood relatives could be found. The same impulse caused blacks to be willing to support children passed from mother to cousin to neighbor, even amid rampant unemployment in modern times.

Gutman's study does not indicate in detail what blacks brought into the city as traditions, conceptions, or means for organizing life. He does, however, provide a solid foundation for this assessment in future studies. Andrew Billingsley, in a review of Gutman's book, sees Gutman in basic agreement with John Blassingame and George Rawick in asserting that blacks have maintained their families and developed a new culture despite all the oppressive conditions they have endured. Billingsley writes of Gutman's study:

> What this shows beyond the fact of family relations involved is the supreme value which Blacks placed on family life and extraordinary efforts that often went into trying to maintain their families.[40]

Billingsley praises Gutman for indicating that not only did black families survive, but black families survived as a basis for a new culture on the American continent. Billingsley concludes:

> Gutman has the data in this book which both sociologists and historians will be turning to in years to come in our effort to understand the resiliency and adaptability of the honor and spirit so well exemplified in the evolution of black families in this country.[41]

There are serious gaps in Gutman's study. He does not give adequate attention to the African background of black slaves or the earliest experience in the West. The obvious place to appreciate the background of the role of kinship in black life is Africa. It follows that he does not appreciate the interior roles that developed within the family and the kin group. Finally, his study makes its mark on the period up to the emancipation and only outlines the future until 1925. So in a real sense the study is a "beginning." The book is invaluable to our study and a great stimulant to vigorous research on the black family. We would be less than honest if we did not say that through almost a decade of fruitful and vigorous research, Gutman fulfills his original intention:

> This is a book about ordinary black men, women and children mostly before the general emancipation but after that time too —a study of enslaved Afro-Americans, their children, and their grandchildren, how they adapted to enslavement by developing

distinctive domestic arrangements and kin networks that nurtured a new Afro-American culture, and how these, in turn,
formed the social basis of developing Afro-American communities, which prepared slaves to deal with legal freedom.[42]

Blassingame rightly refers to the black family, during slavery,
as "an important survival mechanism."[43] And so it has been
until now. After slavery the next most devastating blow, in
my judgment, was the northward urban migration. This
brought blacks in contact with another variety of oppression
in a different socioeconomic and political context. Again the
black extended family often cushioned the cruel social environment and made psychic as well as physical survival possible. The black family like the black church has weathered
many storms in black history. Having framed our discussion
in this chapter in the social history of black churches and
families, we now turn to theological reflection.

CHAPTER V

The Family
of God

Traditionally the black church has been an extended family and the family has been a "domestic church." At the center of this affirmation is the Biblical image of the church as the family of God. We noted earlier that black sociologists and historians have written concerning these two primary institutions, family and church, but still lacking is the black theologian's contribution to point up their interdependence and mutual enrichment. I wholeheartedly agree with James Cone's observation: "We are still waiting for the first in-depth study of the black church from a historical-theological perspective."[1]

In my book *Liberation and Reconciliation* I affirm the importance of viewing the church as a family and the family as a domestic church. I will repeat here two brief paragraphs from that work:

> When we consult the New Testament, we find several "images" of the church. The black theologian will be most interested in those images of the church which convey a sense of unity and especially the notion of peoplehood. Having been exploited by the principle of "divide and rule" by whites, blacks need a cohesive institution to overcome family disorganization and the social concomitants of the same. The black church, at once a religious and community organization, has real possibilities for fulfilling this primary need.

One of the most serious internal problems of blacks is family disintegration. It would be nigh impossible to find a group of people who have been able to survive great hardship without strong familial ties. The destruction of the black family has been deliberate during our sojourn in this country. Although the black man's mere survival is a miracle of grace, it appears that the black church, as "invisible" and as a visible institution, has nurtured this suffering race and kept it alive.[1]

Though my research and reflection would modify some aspects of this statement, the relationship between church and family I affirm with even greater assurance.

A family is the most intimate unit of human relationships. When we use the word "family" our attention is directed to a kinship of persons who have entered into an agreement to love and care for one another across sexual and often generational lines. Our basic definition stems from the traditional view of the family. But even here we see the family as a more comprehensive unit than a married couple and their children. Families of single parents (married but divorced or widowed and unmarried) are clearly included. We also wish to carry along in our purview the extended (or intergenerational) type of family. We would be ill-advised to embark upon a discussion of black families unless the broad view of the family unit were clearly within our range of vision. Oppression has done much violence to the very survival of the black family. We must be prepared to deal with reality. Sanity, health, and wholeness are inherent in our intent. We must be prepared to accept, therefore, the variety, the weakness, and the strengths inherent in the black family tradition.

The importance of the family among an oppressed people takes on a special depth and intensity of purpose. The family is a dike against the adverse sea of circumstances external to it. It can take on a warmth and an acceptance of persons that provides resiliency and strength to face adversity. Of course the reverse is likewise possible. Family life in oppressed conditions can become pathological. Much black-on-black crime, including homicide, occurs within the black family. It

goes beyond spouse conflict and includes the entire family
unit in all its subsystems. The faith of the black church
tradition can enrich the strengths of the black family. At the
same time it can heal the wounds of families beset by pressures from "sinful social structures." Racism has been and
still is a powerful foe to healthy black family life.

I. THE FAMILY OF GOD

The family appears in the Old Testament as a link between
the tribe and the father's house. This distinction occurs in the
later genealogical scheme of the Old Testament (cf. Num.
2:34). The groupings are composed of those who are "one
flesh" and are not limited by external rules. The nucleus of
life is the father's house, where the man is founder of the
house. The wife helps maintain the house. The children all
call him father. The family is all who claim kinship with him.
A family once founded lives and grows as long as there are
descendants, and it reaches back into the past to include all
who have contributed to its strength and unity. I am aware
that feminist theologians may desire to accept another reading. Since I take the Bible seriously, but not literally, I believe
it is in order at this point to acknowledge the cultural-histori-
cal conditions of Hebrew life.

The patriarchal character of family life in Old Testament
times makes the man *ba'al,* master of the family. His is the
ruling will in the community. This does not imply, however,
a one-sided sovereignty. The man is the center from which
strength and will emanate to the whole group which belongs
to him and to which he belongs. Father means both kinship
and authority. The complement of the father's authority is
found in the son. The father's strength is carried on in his
sons. The son acknowledges the father's authority, but also
bears his character. Jesus says, "Love your enemies . . . that
you may be sons of your Father who is in heaven" (Matt.
5:44–45). A man's innermost character reveals what kind of
community or family he really belongs to. In the New Testa-

ment, believers in Christ are referred to as "sons of light" (Luke 16:8), "sons of the resurrection" (Luke 20:36), "sons of the kingdom" (Matt. 8:12). To be a son of the Kingdom demands a continuous inner response to the call of God.

Jesus often presented his teachings in terms of the family (Luke 11:11, 15:11–32, Matt. 21:28–31). Some important references to family in the early church may hark back to his example (e.g., Eph. 6:1ff.). Jesus recognized that the demands of membership in the earthly family may at times clash with the demands of membership in the heavenly family. Jesus' call is very demanding! It transcends and may even break up the earthly family (Mark 1:20; 13:12). One's priorities must be sorted out. The Kingdom comes first. All else demands a "lesser love." And yet devotion to the Kingdom leads to an enriched and fulfilled earthly family life. Jesus, however, reminded his followers that a new community was being called into existence (Mark 10:29f.). He is critical of a blind loyalty to the fathers in the past (Luke 6:23ff.). He goes so far as to say, "Call no man your father on earth, for you have one Father, who is in heaven" (Matt. 23:9). Thus what Jesus is demanding is a radical obedience to the Kingdom of God. All other relationships, including those of earthly kinship, are to be assessed in that context.

In Semitic religion generally, humans and their gods form a social, political, and religious whole. The whole people are referred to as a family of which the god is father in a purely physical sense. Reference is made in Genesis to "the sons of God" marrying "the daughters of men" (Gen. 6:2). They were said to have children and "these were the mighty men that were of old, the men of renown" (Gen. 6:4). But as Semitic religion finds expression in Hebrew personal theism, this anthropomorphism is sublimated. The idea of divine fatherhood emerges, which is entirely dissociated from the physical. Man is created in the image of God. Kinship with God is rooted in nature as well as grace. The God of the creation is the God of redemption. This kinship between God and humans is expressed in the religious nationalism of Israel. Israel's creation by the Father-God (Deut. 32:6; Hos. 11:1) refers to a series of acts by God in history by which Israel was shaped as a nation. Of Israelites as a whole it was said: "You are the sons of the Lord your God" (Deut. 14:1). The individual Israelite, on the other hand, has no right to call himself God's son (II Sam. 7:14; Ps. 2:7; 89:26–27).

In the New Testament we encounter a distinctive transition. God calls his son out of Egypt; for Jesus is viewed not only as the unique Son of God but also as obedient Israel. Jesus is no longer simply a human son (Mark 6:3); he has arrived at his messianic position, "Son of David" (Mark 10:47–48). Jesus refers to himself by the title "Son of Man" (Mark 8:29ff.). This title seems to combine features of the Davidic king and the Servant of the Lord (Matt. 8:20; Mark 8:31, 38). These passages refer to his coming in glory, his suffering, rejection, death, and exaltation, and his present work. Jesus, as Son of Man, is Messiah from heaven who came to identify himself in utter compassion with sinful, suffering Israel, and thus manifested his glory as savior and judge.

Behind this reference to Jesus as Son of Man pointing to his messianic mission is the title Son of God. "Son of God" is rooted in the record of the Jesus of Palestine. It is used at the supreme moments of his baptism and transfiguration (Mark 1:11; 9:7), at his temptation, and on the cross (Matt. 4:3; 27:40). Jesus is recognized as the Son of God by his disciples (Matt. 14:33). Jesus used the word from the Aramaic, *abba,* "father," to sum up his distinct, intimate relation to God (Mark 14:36). His knowledge that God is his father is not abstract. It is embodied in his action and his mission, culminating in his passion and resurrection (Mark 14:36; Luke 24:49). This profound Father-Son relationship is important for our understanding of Christ and his church. This "family language" is an index to our knowledge of the nature and mission of the community which Christ called into being.

II. THE COMMUNION OF SAINTS

Traditional African religion believes in the communion of saints. This belief is inherent in the intergenerational reverence for ancestors. It is a belief which is held across the continent. Therefore it is a foundational belief, directly related to the family system at the heart of African religion.[3]

The Swahili word *ujamaa*, "familyhood," is central to an understanding of solidarity in African societies. Julius Nyerere of Tanzania made the concept famous by shaping it into an African form of socialism. He believes that the destiny of humans is drawn from the traditional African view of society as an extension of the basic family unit. Léopold Senghor of Senegal formed a similar ideology from *Négritude* and developed it into a national program. Thus "family" is central to an understanding of group identity and solidarity in Africa.

While the place of ancestors is essential to understanding the intergenerational fellowship and unity among Africans, it should not be discussed solely in the context of the afterlife. We are more concerned here with the implications of ancestor reverence for understanding the church in the African/Afro-American tradition. How are the "roots" of the African familial and religious life sustained and nurtured in black religious experience?

The concept of the communion of saints is, first, a way of viewing the church as the family of God here and now on the plane of history. It points to a sense of solidarity and unity in the fellowship of believers. It indicates the desirability of a profound sense of kinship. Like an extended family that spans the generations, the church is to be a web of kinship in which everybody is somebody. Blassingame notes evidence of this tie between religion and family in his study of the "slave community." He writes:

> The strong sense of family and community solidarity is indicated by frequent references to relatives and friends by name. Because the church served as the major social center in the quarters there are numerous references to "going to the meeting."[4]

The same writer speaks specifically of religion as "more powerful than the master, engendering more love and fear in the slave than he could."[5] The family was of similar importance. Blassingame observes:

> In his family he [the slave] found companionship, love, sexual gratification, sympathetic understanding of his sufferings; he learned how to avoid punishment, to cooperate with other Blacks, and to maintain his self-esteem.[6]

Throughout the African/Afro-American tradition the family system has been central to understanding the church —its purpose and mission. At the same time religion has been the core of fulfilled family life. Because of severe racist oppression there have been times when the church has been a family for the homeless and times when the family altar has been a domestic church.

It is instructive that scholars could write so much concerning Martin Luther King's concept of the "Beloved Community" without a word about the impact of the black family and church upon his life and thought. In exploring the thought of Dr. King, Kenneth L. Smith and Ira G. Zepp, Jr., have written:

> All of King's intellectual concerns were directly related to the priority he assigned to the Beloved Community. Liberalism and Personalism provided the theological and philosophical foundations of the concept; nonviolence provided the means to attain it; the Christian realism of Reinhold Niebuhr qualified King's initial optimism about the kinds of tactics necessary to move toward it.[7]

King's concept of community is said to be related to millennial hope. It is associated with the Jewish conception of the Messianic Era and the Christian doctrine of the Kingdom of God. The Kingdom of God and the Beloved Community were synonymous in King's thought, according to these writers. Furthermore, King exalted the concepts of creation, prophecies of social justice, and *agapē*. He is said to have gleaned all this from his examination of liberalism, the social gospel, and personalism. Smith and Zepp go on to refer to Harvey Cox's observation that *shalom* is at the heart of King's understanding of community. Cox would locate King's insight more in Biblical categories than in social and political philosophies.[8]

Cox's observation has much wisdom. The Bible is central to King's notion of the Beloved Community. This points to the heart of the matter. The black family and church had a formative influence upon King before he ever went to seminary. The persons who inspired him and taught him during those early years were persons at Morehouse College—e.g., Benjamin E. Mays, George Kelsey, and Samuel Williams. Without the impact of these minister-scholars there would perhaps have been no Martin Luther King as we know him. Furthermore, if it were not for the Christian family—extended family—behind King, he would not have been launched. All who have had the privilege of getting to know his parents are aware of this. We do not deny the refinement King received at Crozer and Boston. But the making of King was the black family and church, both in Atlanta and Montgomery. How could an entire book be written on King's "Beloved Community" and miss this crucial point?

This theme of the Beloved Community was at the center of King's understanding of the church and the Kingdom. It brought the Fatherhood of God and the brotherhood of man together. King observed that social progress is the result of God's help and human effort. I agree with Smith and Zepp as they write:

> The vision of the Beloved Community was the organizing principle of all King's thought and activity. His writings and his involvement in the civil rights movement were illustrations of and footnotes to his fundamental preoccupation with the actualization of an inclusive human community.[9]

King's work was done before black consciousness became an accepted basis for black theological reflection. The impact of the black religious tradition is implicit rather than explicit. But King is such a seminal thinker and activist that we must take seriously his insights concerning the nature and mission of the black church. His work is even more valuable when consciously reflected against the background of the African/ Afro-American church and family tradition. It would be well if the insights of *ujamaa* as viewed by Nyerere could underpin King's "Beloved Community," for instance. The relationship between family and community in home and church is a proper context for a black ecclesiology of worship and action. We will not attempt further development here, but we are aware of fruitful possibilities along these lines.

A further look at the communion of saints points to the church militant. We view the church as it witnesses to the gospel of Jesus Christ amid "principalities and powers." But we are likewise concerned with the healing ministry of the church. Here the gathered and witnessing church as servant is a useful concept. The church as *event* and *institute* presents its servanthood amid the oppressed and oppressors.

In the African/Afro-American religious tradition the "communion of saints" is associated with the "life everlasting." Africans are saying that the "communion of saints" must include reverence for ancestors. The formula "because I am, we are" is a powerful affirmation in Africa. The sense of family extends not only in space but in time. It reaches outward in kinship to the living, but moves backward in time as well. Thus there is a communion between the "living" and the "living dead."

Among Afro-Americans, the family system based on blood ties has been severely assaulted by oppression. New forms of togetherness have moved in to fill the void. Kinship of a type not based on blood ties, forged out of the necessity for survival, has developed in the most unlikely places. Large families often adopt more children on an informal basis. Because of shortages in housing and the high cost of housing, many people from small towns move into the same house or apartment. In a hostile urban setting blacks pool their resources and develop a sense of belonging, a surrogate family. And most black churches assume the character of a large extended family.

With the energy crisis, black families and churches must brace for a new shift in circumstances. The same white suburbanites who herded blacks into the dark ghetto and almost strangulated them, are now themselves "blockbusting" the center cities nationwide. Whatever is most convenient for whites will be done. Blacks will have to adjust to changes planned by the powerful. The powerless, poverty-stricken black masses are like pawns to real estate giants, businessmen, and politicians. Black churches have a responsibility to heal the wounds as well as strive for social justice.

Again the concept of *ujamaa* is highly suggestive of our need for a sense of belongingness. We need to develop a strong group life, a "familyhood," through the black church. Gabriel M. Settiloane provides an African perspective in these words: "Man is man-in-community—*motho ke motho ka batho*—man is man through other people."[10] Herein lies the African "tribal mystique." This does not mean, according to Settiloane, that the individual is submerged in his social environment. It does mean, however, that the locus of any individual must extend as far as the social activity of relationships which constitute it extends. For instance, the dead are believed to be with the living.[11]

Another African theologian, Edward W. Fasholé-Luke, writing on the ancestors, observes:

> We cannot simply say that African ancestors can be embraced within the framework of the universal church and included in the Communion of Saints. . . . [But] the phrase *sanctorum communio* [interpreted] to mean fellowship with holy people of all ages and the whole company of heaven through participation in the holy sacraments, gives us a signpost to the road on which our theologizing should travel.[12]

While black Christians do not seem to hold to this strong belief in ancestors, there is, through their understanding of

Biblical faith, a sustained belief in the reunion of families beyond death. This is dramatically presented on the occasion of the final rites for a deceased relative. The strong extended family instincts of African communal life appears forcefully at the time of bereavement.

A black minister in Minneapolis discussed the manner in which his parishioners respond to death. He observed that because of the small number of blacks in that city and the mixed marriages that took place over a long period, many of the distinctive characteristics of the African heritage had been wiped out. But in spite of that, blacks faced death with dignity and there was a joyous homecoming. At the time of death he perceived a blending of the African religious beliefs and practices with the Christian understanding of the resurrection.

III. HARAMBEE (UNITY) IN THE BLACK CHURCH

The concept of unity, social solidarity, expressed by the Swahili word *harambee,* is essential for the African view of society. This ideal is expressed as a virtue in its own right. It is not just a response to colonialism. Likewise, group loyalty is essential to a sense of peoplehood among blacks. It may become a matter of survival under harsh oppression. This unity will be short-lived, however, unless it is perceived as an intrinsic good. A positive way of grounding this precious ideal is to see it as a part of the continuous experience of blacks in Africa and the New World. It is to be viewed in the context of the family or kinship network at the center of African and Afro-American culture. When affirmed in this manner it can have widespread and lasting importance for the health of persons and the health of people.

Black churches have a golden opportunity to espouse unity in the black community. This is especially true if the black church understands its own nature and purpose in the light of a unity in its own life among its members. The theological self-understanding of the black church must rest with the concept of unity.

The image of the church in the New Testament which best describes this unity is the body of Christ (I Cor. 12:12). Those who view the church as a corporate entity, as the Anglo-Catholics do, have little difficulty with the body image. It is just at this point that blacks, who are mainly Baptists, have their greatest problem. With the stress laid upon adult baptism—which is largely an individual decision—a covenant between individuals and even congregations is not easy to conceive. However, the African understanding—"Because I am, we are"—has an affinity with a Biblical view of the church.

Paul's discussion on the church as the body of Christ needs to be examined against the background of unity, *harambee,* in the African/Afro-American religious and cultural tradition. When Paul uses *sōma* he has in view a living entity over against *sarx,* "the body of death." The body, as Robinson points out, is central to Paul's entire theological scheme:

> The word *sōma* knits together all [Paul's] great themes. It is from the body of sin and death that we are delivered; it is through the body of Christ on the Cross that we are saved; it is into His body the Church that we are incorporated; it is by His body in the Eucharist that this Community is sustained; it is in our body that its new life has to be manifested; it is to a resurrection of this body to the likeness of His glorious body that we are destined.[13]

Paul's experience of conversion may be a clue to the importance of the church as a body. He was converted while he was seeking to stamp out a community. And this community had Jesus Christ as its head. The revelation of God to Paul, which established both his faith and apostleship, was the revelation of the resurrection body of Christ, not as an individual, but as the Christian community. When Paul met Christ, he encountered him in the context of the church. Paul

sees the *unity* of the body as the beginning point of his
discussion. The body is one, but it has many members. Just
as all the members of the body, though many, are one body,
so it is with Christ (I Cor. 12:12). But, on the other hand, the
unity of Christ, as of the human body, does not consist of
one member—it must be many. If there are not many members, the body cannot exist.

Thus the body of Christ, as a human body, is able to be
a diversity without giving up its unity. All the members of
a human body form *one* body despite their number, Paul
asserts. Unity is the basic datum. Multiplicity is subordinate
to unity (I Cor. 10:17). Diversity derives from the preexisting
nature of the unity as organic. This fundamental idea of Paul
is a reversal of the Old Testament meaning of remnant, where
ultimately one represents the many. According to Paul, this
formula was central to the divine operation under the old
covenant, according to which a vicarious minority, progres-
sively reduced by sin, carried God's purpose to the whole
world. The clue to this vicarious "one for the many" is the
doctrine of election (Rom. 9:11). Out of many nations God
chose Israel for his saving mission. But now, according to
Paul, the principle of exclusion is set in reverse. It is not the
one who represents the many. It is instead the many who
represent the one. The many, without limit due to race, class,
or sex (Gal. 3:28), now constitute the one. The unity is inclu-
sive, not exclusive. It is representative and no longer vicarious. The unity is in Christ, who is head of his body, the
church.[14]

This emphasis upon *unity* in the body of Christ is essential
for the black church's self-understanding. The black church
has been particularistic without being exclusive. As George
Kelsey said once, the black church is a *segregated* church,
but not a *segregating* church. Many white churches are both.
While representing the culture, interests, and peculiar needs
of an oppressed people, black churches have reached out
universally to "all sorts and conditions of humans." In this
sense the Pauline understanding, whereby the many repre-

sent the one, states the case for the black church's sense of
mission very well. Another way of stating the case is to see
the black church as both *liberating* and *reconciling* in the
name of him who is Liberator and Reconciler, Jesus Christ.

Our attention has been directed in this chapter to the
context of the black church's self-understanding with the
African/Afro-American religious tradition. We have looked
at the church as the family of God, as the communion of
saints, and as the body of Christ. Along the way we have
paused to describe how these various descriptions of the
church may deepen and enrich the black church's sense of
purpose and mission. We conclude this discussion by asserting that Christ is the head of the church for all Christians.
The church is what Kee calls Jesus' "community of the new
age."[15] From his study of the Gospel of Mark, Kee asserts
that Jesus is God's agent to redeem the whole person and all
of humanity. God has authorized him, as Son of Man, to
inaugurate the new age in the present as well as to bring it
to consummation in the future.

In summary, Kee writes:

> He was the agent of God to summon the community of the new
> covenant, which was to comprise all who discerned in his words
> and work the inbreaking of God's kingdom and who therefore
> sought to live in obedience to his will, to nurture and support one
> another within the community, and to urge all who would hear
> to join the expectant group awaiting God's vindication of Jesus
> as triumphant Son of Man.[16]

CHAPTER VI

The People of God

The image of the church as the "people of God" is highly suggestive for blacks. The Old Testament has long been a favorite portion of the Bible for them. The manner in which God reveals his saving purpose in the history of a people has inherent appeal. Not only the *exodus* but also the *exile* and God's general superintendency of the life of a whole people has a message filled with great meaning for any oppressed people.

I. THE PEOPLE OF GOD IN THE OLD TESTAMENT

Hans Küng provides a moving account of the relationship of God to Israel:

> The Israelites are the chosen people, holy and righteous, just and upright; they know Yahweh, cry to him, seek him, fear and love him, trust and wait for him. God and his people belong together, linked by the covenant which God in his free and powerful mercy had made with this small, insignificant, weak and sinful people: a covenant that is more than a contract, that means a way of life and a community.[1]

Black believers have gleaned from the Old Testament a similar understanding of God as provider. So many experiences of the people of the Old Testament resembled their own that reading these pages of Scripture moved their hearts and wills. Not only Israel's triumphs, but her failures as well, were powerful reminders of the black condition, especially under slavery. Again Küng's words are to the point:

> The history of Israel is a story of repeated failures and betrayals, backslidings and loss of faith; a story of sin. Israel found itself more and more in a crisis, which was also a religious and political crisis culminated in the destruction of the state, an event which was interpreted as judgment and punishment for the sins of the people.[2]

Küng asserts that while the prophets announced God's judgment and rejection of a faithless people, they likewise spoke of mercy. The prophets looked beyond Israel's present misery and expressed hope that God's promises of deliverance would be fulfilled.[3]

Harriet Tubman, enslaved as a Maryland field hand, earned the title "Moses, the deliverer." She was endowed with native intelligence and willpower. But it was her interpretation of the Bible and the depth of her religious convictions that sustained her work. After being beaten by her mistress as a girl, she would be called to family prayers in the house of the slave master. Her prayer was silent and personal. "God make me strong and able to fight." Even as she left the plantation she sang snatches of a Methodist hymn:

> Goodbye, I'm going to leave you,
> Goodbye, I'll meet you in the Kingdom.

Her faith in the God of Israel, the God of Jesus, was so strong that Harriet was able to leave her husband, father, mother, and friends and venture into a hostile world friendless and penniless. She remained in Philadelphia for two years, working and saving her money. She longed to be reunited with her husband, John Tubman, a free "colored" man whom she married about 1844. But when she returned, John had another wife. Her personal loss fired up her determination to give herself to the task of delivering her people. Seven or eight times she returned to the area where she had been a slave to bring away hordes of fugitive slaves. In 1857 she brought away her aging parents. They were too feeble to walk, but she hired a wagon and delivered them anyway.[4] All she did was achieved under the guidance of a profound faith in God. Some might see her as a pathological case. She had been struck in the head by a heavy object thrown by her master at another slave. The blow did affect her brain. She had to be always active or she would fall asleep. She loved physical activity and the direct heat of the sun to keep her blood circulating.[5] However, a more positive power motivated her work as deliverer of her people. This was her religion. The following description of her religious experience merits careful reflection:

> When going on these journeys she often lay alone in the forests all night. Her whole soul was filled with the awe of the mysterious Unseen Presence, which thrilled her with such depth of emotion, that all other care and fear vanished. Then she seemed to speak with her Maker "as a man talketh with his friend"; her child-like petitions had direct answers, and beautiful visions lifted her up above all doubt and anxiety into serene trust and faith.[6]

Harriet Tubman was a woman with great faith in God. She did not trust in her own resources, but leaned on an almighty arm. Her prayers were backed up with action. She conducted fleeing slaves to freedom, even into Canada. She watched over their welfare, collected clothing, organized them into societies and was always preoccupied with plans for their benefit.[7]

This account of Harriet Tubman's role as deliverer of her people is important for several reasons: First, she demonstrates a strong sense of peoplehood. Her desire for freedom is for her race. If she had desired only her own freedom, she would not have returned again and again to set free her faithless husband and her parents. She returned many times at extreme personal risk. Second, the fact that she was a woman is important. She is one of a long list of great black women leaders. Her life illustrates the widespread acceptance of women as leaders among blacks. Her very closeness to her family illustrates the full measure of her devotion to her role as deliverer of her people. Family ties were dear to her. She loved her husband and parents as only a woman could love. And yet, even more, she desired liberty for her people. And, third, her faith in God was the foundation for her dedication to her work of deliverance. She brings a personal embodiment to our consideration of the church as the people of God.

How easy it is for black believers to view their faith-in-community against the background of the Old Testament. The oppression-deliverance formula leaps out of its pages. The black church has always read this message with clarity. It has provided strength and hope.

But there are problems in this traditional reading. We must raise some questions. For example, into what sort of a promised land do we want to be delivered? Are the values of the larger society values we desire to embrace? How are we to view the mission of the black church and the role of the black family? What are our values and goals for these primary institutions which determine the direction of our lives as a people? Why have we not considered the Old Testament more in its message to exiles? We are also people of the diaspora. Since we do not accept, and have not accepted, a return to Africa as our destiny, how do we "learn to sing the Lord's song in a strange land"? What are the perils as well as the promises of our self-description as a chosen people? We could go on with our inquiries, but this would be useless unless we pause for some in-depth discussion. Black theologians have said much about the meaning of the exodus; we have now, in concert with black Biblical scholars, to tackle other pertinent concerns from the Old Testament. If the black situation is a subculture, as Eric Lincoln often reminds us, the black church is a church of exiles and not merely a church of the exodus.

II. THE PEOPLE OF GOD IN THE NEW TESTAMENT

What does it mean to refer to the church as the Israel of God? Paul uses this figure of speech as he writes to the churches of Galatia. These churches were composed largely of Gentiles. The Gentile Christians were often rejected by the "Judaizers" as not being authentic Christians. Paul expanded the notion of the Israel of God to include all Christians, whether Jew or Gentile (Gal. 6:15–16).

God's Israel is one people—based upon God's mercy in the cross of Christ. It is in relation to the people of Israel that the mission of the Messiah is understood. Jesus is sent to Israel (Matt. 15:24) to bring repentance and forgiveness (Acts 5:31). The church knows itself to be addressed by the words: "Hear, O Israel" (Mark 12:29). The God of the church is none other than Israel's God. The fulfillment of all his purposes is shaped by the terms of his steadfast love for Israel. God has entered into a New Covenant, but this is a renewal of the covenant that God established with the house of Israel (Heb. 8:8–13). Paul accepts the "Jewishness" of Jesus. He affirms a solidarity between the God of the Old Testament and the God of the New Testament. The same God fulfills his promises to the same people. Henceforth, the same name could be considered to describe the new community. The Israel to whom the gospel comes and through whom the mission to the world is accomplished is the same Israel to whom the promise had been given.[8]

The New Testament writers called upon the "corporate memory" of Christians. Israel was the name for a story—a story which recalled the inner dynamics of this peculiar society. Christians were asked to recall their communal experience. They were exiles from Egypt, slowly making their exodus through the wilderness to the Promised Land under the leadership of Moses. Another prophet like Moses had been promised by God to deliver Christians from bondage (John 3:14; Acts 3:22).[9] Many episodes by these exiles of old became symbols for the New Israel, the church. In essence we encounter a church of the exodus. A church in the world but not of it. The church is on a pilgrimage, not to an earthly Canaan, but to the Kingdom of God. Christ's church is to be the *transformer* of cultures. The Kingdom, the church's destiny, transcends and suspends the church's mission. The Kingdom is the *mecca* of the church's pilgrimage. As we consider the church as the people of God, we are attracted to those images of the church in the New Testament which point to community, deliverance, and pilgrimage. These images have affinity with the black condition. Similarly the "political" analogies are related to the experiences of black Christians. We have been and are still compelled to struggle for our humanity or accept inhumanity. The black church must be socially active and politically militant. We are encouraged when Paul Minear, writing of the New Testament viewpoint, observes:

> Paul did not evaporate the social structures into pure "Spirit," but he perceived them all as modes of operation of God's sovereign grace, all subject to the power of God to fulfill his promise *in spite of* social intransigence and even *by means of* it.[10]

The possibility of understanding the church as both healing and socially transforming raises an issue concerning the gap that exists between Biblical scholarship and the application of its insights to current problems. We are not referring only to Fundamentalist scholars; we include liberal pacesetters as well. I find this disturbing for many reasons. First, as a black theologian I find that the New Testament provides a forceful message in the quest for social justice. Martin Luther King, Jr., gleaned ample insights from the New Testament to ground his program in the doctrine of love as *agapē*. Howard Thurman relates the message and ministry of Jesus to the disinherited. And so it is and always has been in the black church tradition. Thus, while reading carefully behind the Euro-American pacesetters in New Testament studies, I greatly suspect there is a tendency to spiritualize, privatize, and eschatologize the "social gospel" out of the New Testament.

Second, the Christian missionaries, who served, unwittingly, as "God's colonizers," presented a New Testament faith. They often worked hand in glove with the political and economic exploiters of the people. The deliverance or social justice passages of the Old Testament would have been their undoing. But, instead, a private, spiritual, and otherworldly approach to the New Testament served their purpose well. An Asian student wondered why Chinese Christians did not read the Old Testament with understanding. Upon reflection, the answer was simple. Missionary preachers and teachers neglected to give it adequate attention. In some ways it is a repetition of the experience of blacks under white preachers. It seems logical to inquire: If the church rests finally upon the New Testament, where is its gospel of freedom? Too many Fundamentalists are hemmed in by literalism; while some of the more liberal exegetes are blinded by the Lutheran doctrine of "two kingdoms." My suspicion is that the New Testament is not being allowed to address us with its disturbing clarity and power.

III.   THE LORD'S SONG IN A STRANGE LAND

Basic to the African heritage is the emphasis on togetherness. Individual rights do not crowd out the rights of the group. The sanctity of the individual is tied to the sanctity of the group. All life is fundamentally religious; religion is social and the social is religious.

Africans were brought to the New World with their souls intact. But to enslave them, tribal units were broken up, the members of families were separated, and persons from different tribes, speaking diverse languages, were mixed. In spite of this radical and cruel form of socialization, Africans seemed to have maintained a constant soul life. This is illustrated by their capacity to receive the revelation of God in Jesus Christ. William A. Jones, Jr., writes:

These motley groupings, strangers at first to one another, learned a new language, developed a new dialect, put it together in God's name, and became one of God's new creations, the Black Church. The Black Church was for the slaves, and remains so to this day, the American counterpart of the African extended family.[11]

Jones asserts that there is a closer resemblance between the black church and the Christian communities of the New Testament than is the case with any other church in the Western world. *Koinōnia* derives naturally from its history and life.[12]

The faith of the black church found expression in our ethnohistory. It is seen in the exhortation of black preachers and the simple folktales of unschooled black people. It is found in popular literature and in classic prose, poetry, and drama. In a word, the roots of the faith of the black church are deeply embedded in the soil of black culture.

There is a great deal of contextual theology in the following:

> You are de same God, ah
> Dat heard de sinner man cry.
> Same God dat sent de zigzag lightning tuh
> Join de mutterin' thunder.
> Same God dat holds de elements
> In uh unbroken chain of controllment.
> Same God dat hung on Cavalry and died,
> Dat we might have a right tuh de tree of life—
> We thank thee that our sleeping couch
> Was not our cooling board,
> Our cover was not our winding sheet . . .
> Please tuh give us uh restin' place
> Where we can praise thy name forever,
>   Amen.[13]

God is eternal, the same yesterday, today, and forever. He hears the sinner's cry of repentance and he forgives sin. He is the creator of the elements in the entire cosmic realm. But mankind has a special place in his creative and redemptive plan. God suffers for us. The speaker points to Calvary as proof of God's intention that all might be saved. His prayer concludes with a paean of praise for awakening from sleep to greet the light of another day. And yet he expresses the hope that springs eternal with the assurance of everlasting life. In this simple prayer, a black Christian has expressed much basic theology.

Dr. King recalled walking beside an elderly woman in Selma. He inquired of her if she were tired of walking. Her reply was, "My feets am tired, but my soul am rested." In the midst of great suffering we have been blessed with a sense of humor, "the gift of laughter." We have been able to rejoice in the midst of tears. This sorrow-joy experience is noted in the following excerpt from the spiritual "There's a Little Wheel A-Turnin' ":

> Oh, I don't feel no ways tired in my heart,
> No, I don't feel no ways tired in my heart,
>   In my heart, in my heart,
> Oh, I don't feel no ways tired in my heart.[14]

John J. Jasper (1812–1893) was a slave during his youth. A fellow slave taught him to read. He started reading out of the New York Spelling Book until he was able to read the Bible. Within months he was converted and soon after that he was called to preach. He was no doubt a Biblical literalist innocent of any knowledge of natural science. But his sermon "De Sun Do Move" is a theological credo in itself. He makes no reservation in affirming the creative and redemptive purposes of God. God is Creator, Redeemer, and Judge.

> My Lord is great! He rules in de heavens, in de earth and down under de ground. . . .[15]

Theological insights may likewise emerge from black folklore. Uncle Pleas always prayed, "Oh, Lawd, kill all the white folks, and save all de black." He prayed under a large oak tree every night. The master discovered what he was doing. One night the master got to the tree first and took several rocks up with him. When Pleas prayed this night and repeated his usual refrain three times, the master let two or three rocks fall on his head. Pleas was frightened, for he thought that God was throwing the rocks. He called out, "Look out dere, Gawd! Stop dat th'owing dem rocks. Don't yuh know white from black?"[16]

Several types of black folk expression indicate the manner in which blacks have related their experiences of joy and sorrow to their understanding of faith. Conversely, their understanding of faith has emerged out of these experiences. We have learned to sing the Lord's song in the land of our enslavement. Suppose survivors of the Holocaust were forced to remain where their loved ones suffered and died? The faith of the Jews has often been associated with "land." In the Old Testament it was Jerusalem; while in recent history, it is Israel. But blacks are an essentially landless people with only a "symbolic history" in Africa, and yet through our faith we have learned to sing the Lord's song in racist America.

Our suffering, for the most part, has been profound, but without bitterness. We have sung from the depths:

> Nobody knows the trouble I see,
> Glory, hallelujah.

This statement appears contradictory, but it says something profound. It describes sorrow, joy, and laughter in the midst of tears. We have asked many times, "Is there no balm in Gilead?" But our faith has changed the question mark into an exclamation point. The faith of the black church is a resounding yes! "There is a balm in Gilead to make the wounded whole!"[17]

IV. THE HOUSEHOLD OF GOD

There are several instances in the New Testament where the church is referred to as a "household." The author of I

Peter has used this image (I Peter 4:17). He has identified the house with the Temple, the Kingdom, the race, and the nation (I Peter 2:5–10). The author of Hebrews had similar views. In his mind the household of God over which Jesus presides as a Son harks back to the household in which Moses had been a representative (Heb. 3:1–6).

All this is familiar Biblical imagery. When the Hebrew referred to all humans, it was often as "all the *families* of the earth" (Gen. 28:14). Every person was viewed as a member of a particular family. The family formed the basis of community.

Inseparable from the thought of the family is the father, the patriarch, whose story is the story of his family. Cohesion in society was based upon participation in the continuing life of a common ancestor. The story of the patriarch and the story of the family is one historical saga. But the common story implied more than biological descent—it was more definitive of community. "Common character" was as important as "common blood." Minear writes:

> The homogeneity of the family, the element of kinship, stems from a psychic bond that discloses the fact that contemporary mutualities actually spring from a common source.[18]

Household refers to a community participating in a common tradition—a history flowing from a continuing life of a common ancestor. The New Testament identifies the household of God with the house of Israel and David and with the convenantal promises and the faith granted to the fathers.[19] Johannes Pedersen describes the relation of the patriarch to the tribe as follows:

> He is at the same time the tribe and its father, and to everyone who joins the tribe he thus becomes a father. . . . The patriarchs are neither merely individuals nor the personifications of tribes; they are *fathers* who take part in the life of the tribe. . . . [The father] is not removed by death from his tribe, but continues to live in it and share its adventures. . . . All the great events happening to the tribe are ascribed to [him].[20]

It is well known that ancestors are factors of cohesion in African societies. The deceased remain truly members of the families on earth. They are not closely tied to those who live on earth, but are freed from the restrictions of the physical world. In some sense ancestors are considered to be intermediaries between Deity or the divinities and their offspring. This is a continuation of their earthly functions as heads of families and priests and priestesses of communities. In Africa, it is the general belief that a living father or mother, by virtue of fatherhood or motherhood, can effectively bless an offspring. During every passage in life, therefore, the offspring seeks the parental blessing. It is the duty of parents to help, to ensure the domestic peace and well-being of the community, to exercise discipline, and to serve as guardians of community ethics. It follows that, after death, these same ancestors continue to influence the lives of those left behind. It is generally believed that communion and communication are possible between the living and the ancestors and that the living are under the direct influence of the ancestors.[21]

It is useful to compare the strong family orientation in Israel with the central place of ancestors in African religion. The place of the fathers in Israel is similar to the role of ancestors in Africa. In both cases the life of the community is rooted in the family. The family is at the heart of both religious and community life.

There is, however, discontinuity as well as continuity between the Israel of old and the New Israel. The New Testament image of the church is cosmic and universal as well as particular. Abraham is the father of the faithful, but God, too, is the father for whom all the families in heaven and earth are named. Christians exist as children of God. They have been born into the new creation. Jesus Christ is the living example of their new humanity. Christians are heirs of the Kingdom.[22] In Israel "kinship is a corollary of covenant." In the New Testament the covenant is intended for all humans. Sonship is the fruit of God's salvific work through Christ who enables us to become children of God (John

1:12). The new birth and the indwelling Spirit of God likewise ground the existence and source of sonship in the formation of the new covenant. The household of God refers, then,
to the inner cohesion of this community called church. The
understanding of the church as a household, a family, points
to the reunification of all families.[23]

The church is viewed as a brotherhood. Today we would
refer to it as a fellowship of brothers and sisters. This human
fellowship consisted, in New Testament times, of a unity of
spirit, suffering, sympathy, humility (I Peter 3:8). This fellowship had its basis in the work of Christ. This fellowship
referred to the mutuality of sharing in Christ's sanctification,
his suffering, death, spirit, and Kingdom (Rom. 8:29–30).

The shared relationship Christians had with Christ gave
the word "brother" its meaning. Brothers, as well as sisters,
to Jesus are those who do the will of God (Mark 3:35).
Christians must be willing, if need be, to surrender all existing family ties for family associations with Jesus Christ.
Christ identified with every person in need of food, clothing,
and friendship (Matt. 25:40). Kinship requires a shared humility and immediate action to overcome estrangement. The
household of God is based upon a love that bears, endures,
and hopes all things—it is a sign of the resurrection (I John
3:1 to 5:5).

Olli Alho, a Finnish scholar, has made an important study
of black religion and Christianity. The study is especially
important because of its thoroughness, its objectivity, and its
critical bent. But the insights are decisive as we reflect upon
the church in the Biblical setting as a "household." Black
slaves carved out, under severe oppression, "psychological
space" for their existence. Alho sees the religion of slaves as
a development in its own right. It testifies to the astonishing
creative capacity of blacks, deprived of their geographical,
traditional, and social roots and placed in the midst of an
alien, oppressive culture, to lay the foundations of a new
culture. In this situation they discovered an affirmative identity of their own in the context of community.[24] Alho writes:

The slaves learned from the whites about the transcendental reality of heaven, its ruler and his son; and the history of salvation; but in making these notions their own they attenuated the transcendental aspects by transforming them into something concrete and approachable. They made the sacred history of the Chosen People of the Bible their own, they identified its personages, including Christ himself, with historical figures, and used the same words to describe heaven and countries where men are free. In this way they created a unique land of freedom which was not characterized by being either "this-worldly" or "other-worldly," but by the absence of slavery. This merging of sacred and profane realities was not a linguistic trick made by witty slaves, but a process in the developing consciousness of the community.[25]

We could add much to this from the consciousness of the inside flow of black religious experience. The black church throughout its history has been a household of God. It has provided sanity, meaning, and courageous devotion to persons, families, and communities. Olin Moyd, developing the theme of "redemption" in black theology from black history, has summed up this faith-covenant relationship in the black church as "confederation." By this he means:

The forming of a community, local and universal, of the chosen people of God resulting from their understanding of the will of God, also the practice of a life-style which is consistent with the fulfillment of a covenant relationship with God.[26]

V. THE INTERDEPENDENCE OF FAMILY AND CHURCH IN THE BLACK TRADITION

In this chapter we have centered our reflection upon the church as the people of God. We looked at the concept in the Old and New Testaments. Then we described how the sense of peoplehood among blacks adapted to the harsh realities of life in the New World. The adjustment took place in home and church and the faith of black believers was the secret to this survival and adaptation. We have examined the "house-

hold of God" image also. Again we noted the close affinity
between traditional Israel and Africa concerning both faith
and family life. The creative and constructive reflection on
these themes by the black community was discussed. Within
the context of an understanding of the "people of God" we
have observed the interdependence of family and church in
the black tradition. We now look briefly at that close relationship between the two primary black institutions.

As an oppressed community, blacks sometimes sought
"survival." At other times when more seemed possible, they
sought freedom and meaning for themselves as persons and
as a people. A sizable black middle class is just now emerging
as the result of a long struggle and "affirmative action." But
the mass of uneducated and unemployed blacks are still near
the starting gate. Blacks who are now middle class are often
the first generation of those to be thus fortunate. Many who
were born under fortunate circumstances have offered to help
the less fortunate. Martin Luther King, Jr., Andrew Young,
and Julian Bond are persons in this category. These persons,
and many like them, emerged from strong family and/or
church backgrounds. Two of these, King and Young, elected
to serve the church as ministers. It was through the black
church that they discovered a larger ministry. While remain-
ing loyal to their black roots, they went on to serve the entire
human race.

We are asserting that what has happened in the black
family affects what happens in the black church. The church
in the black tradition has been an extended family; while the
family, in many instances, has been in fact a "domestic
church." Church and family together have nurtured our suffering race and preserved us through all the ordeals of our
history. Altar and "family altar" have provided succor and
healing. But they have also fired the black saints for battle
against social evils. The holistic nature of the black Christian's understanding of religious experience has served us
well. We have maintained a strong commitment to personal
evangelism, which has strengthened rather than weakened

our quest for social justice. In the self-understanding of the black church, we have absorbed the self-identification of Israel as a "corporate personality." We learned early that individual black Christians are no match for sinful social structures. We knew this long before Walter Rauschenbusch and Reinhold Niebuhr wrote their definitive studies. Our sense of peoplehood has African roots. "Familyhood" is religious and secular, secular and religious. What has been central in our religious heritage is worthy of Biblical and theological discourse. It is at the heart of soul culture.

CHAPTER VII

The Black Church's Ministry — Priestly and Prophetic

The black church is obligated to minister to black families. There are two aspects of this ministry, the priestly and the prophetic, which in no way denies its holistic character. The distinction, made for the sake of discussion, is based upon the need for clarity. The *priestly* ministry of black churches refers to their healing, comforting, and succoring work. The *prophetic* ministry involves its social justice and socially transforming aspects. The bridge between these is the relation between love and justice. The interdependence of persons in their *liberating* and *reconciling* relationship is the means for holistic ministry to persons and to a people. In an oppressed community, the *priestly* and *prophetic* aspects of ministry are but two sides of the same coin. Personal concerns relate to social concerns and social realities determine the limits of personal freedom.

Eric Lincoln has provided a helpful perspective on black institutions. He asserts that the meaning of being black in America is to be "debarred from certain significant experiences, and to have those experiences which are available filtered through an alternative set of screens which may determine a different perception and registration of reality from that common to the larger society."[1]

Lincoln explains that the dominant culture tends to codify

its appraisal of minorities, and in turn that appraisal becomes formative:

> The ramifications of external appraisal at the hands of the "host culture" are far reaching, for among other things, it means that all of the significant institutions which undergird the ontological understandings of a contingent community are either ignored or presupposed as consistent with those of the external evaluator. ... The conventions of the overculture have played the dominant role in the architecture of particular black institutions—as in the case of the black family.[2]

I. PRIESTLY MINISTRY TO BLACK FAMILIES

A. The Black Church's Need for a Theology for Ministry

It is just not true that activism is sufficient in itself. The black church needs a theology both for its self-understanding and for its sense of mission. We need to know not merely that we should *act;* we need to know *why* we should act. Theology and ministry are inseparable.

This theology for the black church must be more than a lay version of theology. It must take seriously the black experience of religion. There are several books written by black writers which help us to describe the nature of the black religious experience. Among these are Howard Thurman, *The Negro Spiritual Speaks of Life and Death;*[3] Benjamin E. Mays, *The Negro's God;*[4] Joseph A. Johnson, Jr., *The Soul of the Black Preacher;*[5] W. E. Burghardt Du Bois, *The Souls of Black Folk;*[6] Cecil W. Cone, *The Identity Crisis in Black Theology;*[7] and Henry J. Young, *Major Black Religious Leaders 1755–1940.*[8] There are other valuable studies which attempt to explore the black religious experience from some particular angle such as mysticism, literature, homiletics, or theology. These studies and others like them provide the vital raw material for the development of a black church theology.

C. Eric Lincoln has said that we cannot depend upon white theologians to provide theology for the black church. The black church must do its own theological reflection:

> The black church has traditionally relied upon a "preached" theology. . . . Now that era may be past. The Blacks of this generation, and possibly for generations to come, are going to write their own theology in the light of their circumstances and their needs. A white Jesus, whether preached, taught or implied by cultural habits, simply won't do. In a society like ours, *he can't do anything for black folk!*
>
> A white church that is painfully adjunctive to institutionalized racism—the consequences of which are devastating the whole society—can't do anything for black people. It can't do anything for itself.
>
> White theology suffers mortally from the sin of omission. It has sent its theologians to study in Europe where the problem isn't, or imported the best European theologians to bring us the light, but not for *our* darkness.
>
> In consequence, American theology has had few words to speak to *our* condition. White theology has not done anything for black people except ignore them.[9]

Lincoln's statement is consistent with his overview of the black condition based upon his study of the history and sociology of the black experience. Blacks did not come to America minus culture. Due to oppression based on race, they have had their destiny defined for them by the dominant culture. But they have carved out for themselves adequate space to develop a survival culture. Black churches and families have been vital instruments in the development of a healthy and viable people. But Lincoln—unlike some other black religious scholars who have been heavily influenced by the social sciences—sees a great need for developing a black church theology. The fact of "omissions" in white theology makes it imperative that black theologians fill the gaps for the black church's self-definition and ministry to black people.

B. Theology and Ministry to Blacks

Many black activists, including many ministers, see black theology as excess baggage. People have said to me that Leon Sullivan and Jesse Jackson don't need a theology, for they are doing an effective job without it. Our view is that black theology has made its case whether any particular church leader accepts or rejects it.

Some powerful church leaders have taken a forthright stance against black theology. A case in point is Joseph H. Jackson, president of the multimillion-member National Baptist Convention.[10] On the other hand, Joseph A. Johnson, Jr., a bishop and Biblical scholar in the C.M.E. (Christian Methodist Episcopal) Church, is producing his own version of what he calls "a black Christian theology." Johnson writes:

> A new understanding of the Christian faith emerged out of the black Christian witnessing community. . . . One's experience of the life of faith comes from participation in the community of faith and the form of this experience will vary widely depending on what the racial group brings to the faith.[11]

Bishop Johnson's work is very encouraging. He is dedicated to a version of black theology which underscores effective preaching and ministry in black communities. His knowledge of Scripture is considerable and he has been an effective church leader for many years. He has challenged all black theologians to provide a theology for ministry in black churches. Joseph R. Washington, Jr., a religious ethicist and social scientist, puts the matter this way:

> It is incumbent upon the black church to discover what its ministry, indeed, its special ministry has to be. When this discovery has been made then it is incumbent upon the black church to see that that ministry takes place wherever black people are.[12]

All movements for social change require an ideology. Thought and action are related. When churches are involved in social transformation, we must be concerned with an ade-

quate theology for *praxis.* Martin Luther King, Jr., spent
many years reflecting upon a theological ethic for the movement he later was called upon to spearhead. Many activists
in the black church today are still indebted to King's thought
as a basis for action. Black churches need not be totally
dependent upon others to provide them with a theology for
any purpose. We need to mine our own African/Afro-Ameri-
can heritage incessantly as an alternative to depending upon
others to do our thinking. Church leaders and religious activists need theological foundations for ministry. Black theologians and church leaders must no longer work at cross-pur-
poses—they must reinforce each other. We must move from
action to reflection and from reflection to action.

C. The Black Church Confronts Black Suffering

A people who know the meaning of suffering from long
experience with it need a faith that brings comfort and assurance. The tears of Jeremiah, the anguish of Habakkuk, and
the patience of Job have tested and challenged our faith
through the long night of oppression. The Judeo-Christian
faith, filtered through the suffering of blacks, has developed
into a tower of strength for survival and meaning. Their
understanding of God and affirmation of trust in him has
steeled black believers against the adversities of life heaped
upon them by an unjust and inhuman system of oppression
based upon racism. Much of the emotionalism in black worship is therapeutic. It releases the tension that oppression
forces upon black people. It is often an aid to psychological
health in a racially pathological situation in which black
people struggle for sanity. Obviously an experience of worship, theologically grounded, should be more than a release
of tensions, but this may properly be included.

Black religion provides meaning in an otherwise meaning-
less situation. Our theological task is to supply a theological
underpinning for meaning in black life. Black churches are
now experiencing a great influx of black youth because of the

popularity of gospel music. These youth view gospel music as a part of a discovery of their black heritage. But the underlying reason for the enchantment with the "gospel sound" may be a profound search for purpose and value in life. Gospel music is emotional and otherworldly. It has little if anything to do with finding meaning for life in a hostile world. Unless we are able to anchor the celebration in Biblical faith and personal and social ethics, our success story will have a short history.

The spirituals came out of our slavery experience. They had the advantage over gospel music of being both this-worldly as well as otherworldly. Perhaps it would be useful for us to sing spirituals along with gospel songs and to seek to interpret both—that is, to provide the social-historical context as well as the Biblical and theological message of both forms of black music. In addition much black "secular" music is full of social criticism and religious meaning.

Much of the priestly content for black church theology is hidden in the black prayer tradition. Prayer in the black church unearths the tragic soul life of a suffering race. Prayer reaches into the depths of the human spirit—even to its preconscious level. But prayer is also conscious and potent with meaning for the oppressed. Strength from black prayer is shared by members in black fellowship. Many black Christians are sustained and nurtured by prayers of fellow pilgrims delivered at the midweek prayer meetings. Some traditional worship services begin with a prayer meeting. Black church theology has yet to unlock and interpret the raw materials for theology in the prayer life of blacks. Along with our study of slave conversion narratives and confessions of faith, we need to know what the "unexpressed" longings of blacks in the secret places of the heart have uttered before God. While we arouse black Christians to action against social evils, we need to know what spiritual resources have held the pieces of life together and sustained a suffering people through its dark night of suffering. Prayer is the bridge between the black church and family. There is a direct connection between the church altar and the family altar in the black tradition.[13]

Black church theology must not give all its attention to social transformation. The existential taproots of religious experience provide morale and meaning. Without healing in our personal lives we will not be prepared for liberation. Strong families as well as warm fellowships provide the matrix for the comfort, healing, and belongingness that make life whole.

Our faith in a God who enters into our joys and sorrows has brought us to this day. We have believed that God suffers but is not weak. The "crucified God" is an "able" God. We do not ask, "Is God a white racist?" We believe that God is loving and just. We attribute our suffering based upon racism to the injustice and cruelty of other human beings. Edward P. Wimberly states the case well:

> God is able to enter into our pain and suffering caused by the devastating powers of evil. But God can do more than this. He can help us find resources to help us live meaningful and triumphant lives in spite of the threatening hand of suffering. . . . Our God may suffer, but like all suffering, it is only temporary. God is able.[14]

All humans suffer because life has its moments of pain and disruption—physical, psychological, or spiritual. But victims of structural oppression bear a double portion of suffering. Much of their anguish is caused by pain inflicted upon them (individually or as a group) by other human beings. Oppressed people need an adequate faith to sustain them as they face the reality of their lives as persons, as families, and as a people—hence the peculiar mission of black families and churches.

D. Ministry to a Black Family Facing a Personal Crisis

Much pastoral care in the black church tradition is done through preaching, teaching, and pastoral conversation. The informal worship in many traditional black churches provides opportunity for group counseling and therapy to occur.

Furthermore, the black church is often much like an extended family of care, sharing, and fellowship. It is a place where one belongs, is affirmed, and finds acceptance. The pastor is regarded, in many instances, as a father or mother. Members relate to the pastor much as they do to a parent. Even a young pastor may be thus regarded by older people. The relation between pastor and people in the black church needs careful attention. It may promote or stunt growth in people. If the relation of pastor to people becomes "paternalistic" it can cripple people so that they will not be able to face reality. On the other hand, the close kinship ties can provide a real opportunity for nurturing persons toward spiritual maturity as wise parents do for their offspring.

Henry Mitchell describes the process of evangelism in the black church with the image of the extended family in view. He believes that new members should be attracted to membership in a black church by the family atmosphere of the fellowship:

> When a church has become the family of God, the next step is to lead its new members by adoption to an awareness that they are literally God's children, with all that entails. The purpose of new Christians is not statistical and financial, nor is it to gain support for a written creed. The purpose is to help them to sense that they are children of God and to act as befits His children, living out that commitment in the context of the very family of God.[15]

What Mitchell is saying is in line with the thesis of this book. His focus on evangelism is related to what we are saying here about the nature of pastoral care. We must bear in mind what can be done and what cannot be done in keeping with the resource limitations of many black churches. This means that the pastor needs to be perceptive in transferring some responsibility for pastoral care to other capable persons in the "extended family." This the pastor will do in addition to farming out some responsibilities to professional persons or agencies.

Edward P. Wimberly has written a definitive study of pastoral care for black churches. I have been greatly assisted by this book as well as through personal conversation with the author. According to Wimberly, pastoral care has four functions: healing, sustaining, guiding, and reconciling. He emphasizes the black church's ministry to families. Wimberly is realistic. He sets limits to what may be expected as far as healing and reconciling are concerned. The strong emphasis, he believes, has been the black church and the black pastor's approach to sustaining and guiding. Healing and reconciling may result, but these are not predominant in pastoral care in the black tradition.

Wimberly further notes that a family has a network of subsystems; these include the relations between spouses, siblings, in-laws, etc. When a crisis develops in the family, the pastor needs to get to the cause of the trouble. The root cause could be in any one of the several subsystems. This root cause could result in the breakdown of the entire family situation. If one considers only the secondary causes, ministry will not be effective. He also believes that role-playing in counseling is native to the black heritage and can be used effectively in leading persons and families out of crises.[16]

We must be prepared to minister to the human situation as it is—not as we would like it to be or as it used to be. Recently, as I conducted a family life conference in a local church, I realized I could not limit my concerns to "a healthy marriage." Among those participating was a woman with two children, who was recently separated from her husband and had moved in with her mother. We need therefore to prepare for ministry to many different kinds of families, to offer help wherever it is needed.

The black pastor will often find an opportunity to help in family crises. There are always opportunities to break the "fatalism" inherent in many family situations. The black minister, as head of the black church, which is an extended family, is in an awesome position. Here one can be most successful and yet this opportunity can lead to tragic failure. One who has personal sexual weaknesses, or who does not have skills for counseling or contacts for referral, or who does not know when to let go, has entered deep waters in a paper boat. However, the pastor who is wise, mature, and skillful, and has the sensitivity to deal with family crises, finds this one of the most fruitful and rewarding aspects of ministry in the black church. The black church can be the context in which much healing can take place. Under the leadership of an able pastor, the black church fellowship can nurture a family in crisis and make it whole again. In doing this, part of the priestly ministry of the black church will be fulfilled. The black church has no greater mission than its ministry to black families. Our personhood and peoplehood depend upon the future and strength of black families.

II. PROPHETIC MINISTRY TO BLACK FAMILIES

Ministry to black families has to take under review the external social, political, and economic factors that relate to black family crises. For an oppressed community, most personal problems cannot be isolated from social causes. For good reason the black church has to direct its ministry to the whole person in all of his or her relationships. Blacks brought with them from Africa a holistic concept and practice of religion. Biblical faith, as understood by blacks, undergirds and deepens this understanding of religion. Therefore, the Christian faith as understood in the black church tradition is rightly concerned about the whole person and all of life. Some will say correctly that this is not what they observe in *all* black churches. My rejoinder is that those churches not ministering to the whole person in all of life are not true to their heritage, and it would be well if they would consider that heritage. They will find in it much that would lead them to a profound understanding of the Christian faith itself.

The black church has as one of its greatest tasks the "liberation" of the family. It will be unfortunate if blacks begin to participate in male-female conflicts in imitation of others on issues that are not crucial to the welfare of the black family. The problems that confront the relationship between black men and women are serious. But they must be seen for what they are and dealt with in that context. Most black families are solidly within the black subculture essential to black survival. We will be defeated if we give our attention solely to mainstream problems and bypass those concerns peculiar to the black condition. In the following brief sections I will describe some of the problems faced by black women, men, and children, and the family unit as a whole.

A. Black Motherhood

The choice of "motherhood" as a topic under which to discuss the black woman does not imply that the sole purpose of black women is to be mothers, that is, to have children. Our concern here is with black families. Black women are often single parents as well as partners with black men in a family unit. Thus we are considering black women as mothers in the present discussion.

Michele Wallace has exploded the "myth of the black superwoman," but at the same time she has leveled a broadside at all black men.[17] Her treatment of the myth that black women are self-sufficient and can live a full life without the love and companionship of a man is an important contribution. She has courageously expressed a woman's point of view concerning a subject that needs in-depth discussion. What has been accepted as a given of the black woman's makeup may well be an adjustment to the harsh reality confronting black women. Wallace may have given too much attention to the white woman as the black man's alternative to black women. The fact is that most black men who have turned to white women were first in love with black women and often married to one. The other fact is that there was serious trouble between black men and women long before white women were readily available. A further fact needs mentioning. Many black men who have left their families for a white companion have not made it with white women either. It may be, that what we really ought to deal with is the root cause of the male-female conflict within the black situation. Both men and women may share some of the blame.

Wallace views most black women as Amazons or as imitations of "ladies" in white society. In either case they are not true to their own feelings and desires. She does not spare her black sisters and criticizes some of the best-known black women. Angela Davis, according to Wallace, built her life in the black liberation movement around the black male as "political prisoner." She even fell in love with one who considered black women enslaving.[18] Wallace writes:

> Angela Davis, a brilliant, middle-class black woman, with a European education, a Ph.D. in philosophy, and a university appointment, was willing to die for a poor, uneducated black male inmate.[19]

Nikki Giovanni receives even harsher treatment. Giovanni was the reigning poetess of the black liberation movement during the 1960's. According to Wallace, she mainly supported black men, suggesting that they return to their roots and partake in the revolution for black liberation. In consequence of the message of her poems, Giovanni is said to have shut herself off from black women while black male poets had a tendency to ignore her. She became an unstable opportunist. Wallace writes:

> She began to speak positively of the church and to focus more on having babies and loving the black man. . . . She herself had a baby and refused to disclose the name of the father. Early in the seventies she told young black women to become mothers because they needed something to love. She also told young black people that school was useless and a waste of time—despite her own years of education at Fisk University. Soon after, she backed away from these positions, amending her original statement about having babies to you-should-only-have-one-if-you-could-afford-to-take-care-of-it like

she could, and actually encouraging Blacks to go back to school.[20]

Wallace views Davis and Giovanni as representing the best that black women were allowed to offer. Davis suggested that you support the black man in the black liberation movement—if need be go to prison with him. Giovanni said "have a baby." According to Wallace, her visit to Riker's Island penitentiary revealed the bitter consequences of Davis' advice. She met black female prisoners who were there because of black men they loved. The "mass" black woman was there because she supported a pimp, a dope supplier, or a robber. But the political black women were there for the same reason—support of a black man. The results of Giovanni's advice to black women is also evident. "By the time she advised them later to first make sure they had enough income to support the child, a lot of women were already on welfare."[21]

As we examine what Wallace has to say about the motherhood of black women, the more one wonders concerning the future of the black family. Motherhood outside of marriage and often independent of marriage vows is nothing new. This is to state a fact and not to make a value judgment. In the 1930's, E. Franklin Frazier wrote about what he called "unfettered motherhood." Frazier stated that many a black woman refused to be married to the father of an unborn child, "because she did not want to be bothered with a husband." Frazier went on to say: "She was not ashamed of her pregnancy, she was proud of the fact that she was to become a mother and had been congratulated by the women in the neighborhood on her fertility."[22]

According to Frazier, motherhood and marriage were two different things. Motherhood was usually accepted with seriousness. Frazier writes, "The unmarried mother is as sensitive as the legally married mother to what is expected of the woman as a mother." The following conclusion is instructive:

Motherhood signifies maturity and the fulfillment of one's function as a woman. But marriage holds no such place in the esteem of many of these women.[23]

There is a direct line from the past to the present. The government's National Center for Health Statistics reported that in 1976 the number of black children born out of wedlock exceeded 50 percent of all black births. This is said to represent a 50 percent increase over a thirteen-year period. I am aware that this report is controversial and that these figures need to be carefully examined. Even if the statistics are partly wrong, the black family is still in serious trouble. June Brown, a black columnist of the *Detroit News,* raised the issue: "If the strength of a race depends upon the strength of its families, then the black race is getting weaker every year."[24]

If motherhood is sacred and independent of marriage and if black women, past and present, view the black man only as a means to childbirth, we need to ask why. This, I believe, is related to the black man's lack of a sense of obligation beyond begetting children. If men are allowed to beget children freely, without any sense of love or responsibility, this is not good for the woman, man, or child, and it will eventually be the undoing of the black family and the black race.

Some of us may have assumed that black women have babies out of wedlock because they desire this fulfillment under impossible circumstances as far as marriage is concerned. But we have another problem to consider. Is this apparently instinctive separation of the role of motherhood and wife a real problem? Is it possible that black women, even in marriage, separate the roles to such an extent that the spouse is expendable when children are born? Michele Wallace asks why so many black women choose this type of motherhood. Many are saying that if they do not marry by thirty, they will have a baby anyway. She observes that this trend is old, but there is a difference now which is disturbing

—it is widespread and increasing. The cause does not seem to be love for children. If these women refuse to consider marriage to the father of the child, even if he is willing and worthy, it cannot be out of love for black men either. She writes:

> Whereas unmarried black women with babies have usually lived with extended families, these women tend to brave it alone. Whereas the black women of previous generations have generally married soon after the baby was born, these women may not and often say they do not wish to. Whereas the practice of having babies out of wedlock was generally confined to the poorer classes of black women, it is now not uncommon among middle-class, moderately successful black women. A woman may pick a man she barely knows. She may not even tell him he is going to be a father or permit him to ever see the child.[25]

While there is much in Wallace's book to which I would take exception, I fully appreciate the issues raised here. Motherhood outside of wedlock—or even motherhood within marriage, when it is isolated from a total family relationship—is cause for concern. The concern is intensified if one has real interest in the future of the young in a pluralistic society hostile to the well-being of black people. We need to ask, How do we make "motherhood" a part of a healthy and whole family relationship? Not only does the black woman need someone to love, the black man has the same need and the black child needs the love of mother and father. Circumstances will lead to some single-parent black families. Some of these single-parent families may be headed by fathers who will love and care for the young. But as far as possible these should be exceptions based only upon necessity.

What we have discussed here is not a general attack upon black women; rather it is a call for self-examination in the light of history and in the face of great odds which a racist society has imposed upon all blacks. So many problems are a part of the black woman's experience. Some of these are loneliness, scarcity of eligible black men, inadequate sex education, the unfaithfulness and brutality of some black men, and a larger society insensitive in its welfare services. The miracle is that there are so many lovable and caring black women who have found a way to cope with the harsh realities of life, who suffer without bitterness.

Inez Smith Reid, in a study for the Black Women's Community Development Foundation, interviewed black women nationwide. The entire study is worth careful examination, but she provides us with a look at some adaptations black women are making in face of the desire to be liberated. She warns that "liberation can be a trick bag."[26] She provides this crucial observation:

> While some in the black community may decry traditional marriage and opt instead for mutual understanding or simply living together in lieu of a formal marriage ceremony, all in the name of freedom, the question remains—as posed by many women— will this represent freedom or liberation from responsibility? That is, will men with increased freedom feel no compunction about walking out on women and/or ignoring the needs of children they have helped create? Moreover, while some view the pill as a liberating force, in the sense that freedom from a constant process of nine month pregnancies may mean more time for "revolutionary" activities, others look upon it as an oppressive mechanism which through evil side effects not only can incapacitate one in terms of performing activities for the black struggle, but also effectively preclude the production of additional troops for the "revolution." Furthermore, polygamy may indeed allow more freedom to experiment and experience different life-styles. Yet it is equally apparent that the introduction of polygamy . . . into Black American society may also cause personal and psychological conflict as well as augment the economic strains on black men.[27]

B. The Black Man: Fathering

Black men have a bad reputation as fathers. This statement is not intended as an absolute condemnation of all black fathers. Many black men are serious about their fatherly responsibilities. Indeed, some have worked themselves to an early death in order to fulfill their obligations to a family. Black fathers have also shown deep affection for their children and have spent considerable time caring for the young. There are enough caring fathers to provide hope that more men may be encouraged to assume this important role. I was personally blessed with such a father—we continue to share precious moments together. His fathering has challenged me to assume responsibility for my family.

Edward V. Stein notes that there are two aspects to fathering—the biological and the psychological. The biological aspect is brief, easy, and satisfying. The psychological part is a lifetime endeavor—it has "peaks and valleys of anguish that would try a god."[28]

Stein points out that science has reduced the biological aspect of fathering to a peripheral dimension. Through artificial means, a few males could supply enough sperm to repopulate the whole earth. Psychological fathering, on the other hand, is greatly needed. It is an individual responsibility and is needed now more than ever. Stein refers to a study of seven suicidally depressed patients in San Francisco General Hospital. The patients ranged from adolescence to age fifty-nine. All had lost a father in childhood, either through divorce, desertion, or death. Stein does not conclude that therefore all suicidal patients are suffering from the absence of the father in the family. He does, however, draw the reasonable conclusion that fathering is psychologically important.[29]

A student of mine in a doctoral program admitted that I had become for him a surrogate father. He was a brilliant student who had fought his way through all types of personal and social difficulties. He had been involved in the underworld in a major urban center. He had experienced drugs and promiscuous sex, and had known life at its worst. He was reared by a mother, along with several sisters. Before his drunkard father deserted the family, the boy had promised to kill him. After a radical experience of conversion he was able to accept his father and visit him. Though he is extremely close to his mother and sisters, he indicated that he often needed a father and especially so in his early adult life. When I met him, he opened up his life to me as if I were his own father. A few weeks before I met him, I had lost my son in an automobile accident. The feeling was mutual—I needed a surrogate son and he needed a surrogate father. A sense of kinship developed between us and continues. There is nothing unusual about this in the black tradition. This case does illustrate concretely the importance of the fatherly role.

Nathan Hare writes about "the frustrated masculinity" of the black male. Black men, he says, are preoccupied with the effort to be masculine. Traditionally, they were not even able to protect their wives and daughters from white men. Moreover, black males are often unable to be good providers. Even if they are hard workers and gainfully employed, their wives often make more income. The tension between a nonprofessional husband and a professional wife may be severe. Sports do not necessarily compensate for the need for masculinity felt by black men. White racists have used the myth of the black man's sexual power to fan the flames of race hate. The black male, according to Hare, has been an object of curiosity to many white women. Society has tried "to stifle or minimize the masculinity of the Negro male in actuality, sometimes even by outright castration."[30] Some black males are so frustrated by the social pressures under which they live that they reject work altogether "and turn to pimping as a compensatory exploitation of the female."[31] Alvin F. Poussaint, a noted black psychiatrist, asserts:

> Whites' reactions to the sexual mythology which they have created have wreaked havoc on the black man's psyche—distorting his self-image and creating his anxieties. Because whites have feared black male sexuality, they have made every effort to make the black man impotent.[32]

Black men should never confuse sexual liberation with political liberation. In fact, the pursuit of the white woman

in some cases could be a compensatory action. This is true
if the black man defines his worth, values, and virility only
in terms of his association with white women. On the other
hand, it is disturbing that many of the "high achievers"
among black males turn to the white woman for companionship. Part of the reason may lie in Robert Staples' observation: "Some middle-class men turn to white women who fit
even better the model of femininity as set forth in this country."[33]

Staples is on target as he continues:

> [Black] women, to a large extent, are victimized by the fact that
> the very same characteristics they need to obtain career mobility
> (aggressive, strong achievement drive) are the ones which make
> it difficult to attract and hold a man. Thus, they are often placed
> in the position of a forced choice between career and marriage.
> And men place them in this position by their insistence on
> women playing supportive, noncompetitive roles.[34]

Also the scarcity of available black men is crucial. Between the ages of fifteen and thirty the mortality rate of black
males is higher than that of black females. War, homicide,
and suicide are high on the list of causes of the shortage of
black males. Almost a half million black males are behind
bars, an estimated one third of black men in the inner city
have a drug problem, and 25 to 50 percent are unemployed.[35]

It appears that what slavery did not do to remove the
father from the black family, urbanization did. Staples writes:

> In the South ... men *helped* to provide for their families. As they
> came to the urban North, materialistic values gained ascend-
> ancy. The symbols of manhood, sexual conquest, dominance of
> women, etc., became important to black men because they
> lacked the real symbols—political and economic power.[36]

Thus we come to the real issue—the manner in which the
powerlessness of the black male in the structures of society
has had a negative influence upon black male-female relationships and, as a result, upon the black family. What we have
written here is a reminder of the awesome task before those

who desire to minister to the fathers or fathers-to-be in black families. The work of Jesse Jackson of PUSH is essential. He has correctly challenged black males to responsibility in the black family. But we must see this challenge in the context of the oppressive racial structures of the larger society. Black men and women must see their roles and rights in relation to each other as they seek to save the family.

C. The Black Child

It is difficult to grow up today. Any child has extreme temptations and conflicts to confront. The black child faces obstacles far beyond the usual concerns of childhood. It is remarkable that we have such a large number of wonderful black youngsters.

Any problem affecting children in general can be greatly enlarged when seen in relation to the black child. The manner in which divorce relates to the welfare of children is a good example. All children are disturbed by the disruption of a stable family. When divorce is seen in relation to child custody and support, the black child receives a crushing blow. The increase in divorces means that more children live in single-parent households during their formative years.

A study released by the United States Census Bureau entitled "Divorce, Child Custody and Child Support" suggests that the nation's divorce rate has climbed from 2 per 1,000 in 1940 to 5.1 per 1,000 persons in 1976.[37] By 1978 some 19 percent of families with children were maintained by one parent—17 percent by the mother and 2 percent by the father, up from 7.5 percent and 1.1 percent in 1960.

Black families were hit severely by this trend. The proportion of mother-only families grew from 21 percent to 45 percent between 1960 and 1978; among whites the increase was from 6 percent to 13 percent. Families maintained by the father only in the same period grew from 1 percent to 1.7 percent among whites and from 2.3 percent to 2.7 percent among blacks.

The support issue is just as upsetting. Black women constituted 28 percent of women eligible for child support, but only 12 percent of these black women received child support payments. The study showed that 45 percent of divorced mothers who had finished college received child support; 29 percent for high school graduates and 11 percent for non high school graduates. This account of the relationship of education to child support clearly indicates that black women and their children were severely hit by this discrepancy.

This study gives a dismal picture of the plight of the black child of divorced parents. It is extremely limited for our purpose. It does not treat the situation of unwed parents and their offspring. It does not look at the black child in foster homes or institutions. It does not deal with the black child in criminal institutions. The poor black child does not have the benefit of the best opportunities for reform and is often punished to the full extent of the law. Black children, especially males, are often victims of police brutality. Others are exploited by some of their own people—such as dope peddlers and prostitutes. The plight of many black children is difficult. The black child is in need of all the support that parents, relatives, and churches can possibly give.

Two black psychiatrists, James P. Comer and Alvin F. Poussaint, have provided some useful perspectives on the black child in white America. The first problem discussed is how black children have had to cope with white oppression. They write:

> In the past, black children were taught the rituals of servitude and docility from the time they could talk. . . . Today the black child is still made to feel inferior to whites. From his earliest days he senses that his life is viewed cheaply by white society and that he enjoys little protection at its hands.[38]

Secondly, the black child must learn how to adapt to society in a manner to gain self-esteem.

> The black child has been forced to live in two cultures—his own minority culture and the majority one. He has had to teach

himself to contain his aggression around whites while freely expressing it among blacks. Some people call this a survival technique.[39]

Finally, the black child has had to resort to those tactics which are necessary for self-preservation. Comer and Poussaint observe:

> Over the years black children have become skilled in the use of a variety of techniques in their struggle for survival and well-being in a hostile and unjust society. They have had to learn to be practical as well as cunning. They have had to learn how to win some acceptance from belligerent whites. Black children as a result have often assumed the responsibilities and burdens of adulthood at a far too early age. Many have had little of what we call a childhood. In the black world adolescence starts early in life, and unlike most white youngsters, many black children do not enjoy the luxury of a period of playtime and learning which extends into their late teens.[40]

D. Family Liberation

What we are attempting to say here is related to how all the problems triggered by institutionalized racism affect the black child and the entire black family. Books and essays by white scholars are helpful as problems are expressed in individuals and families.[41] But they do not deal adequately with the sickness of the society as a structural evil. We do not have time to treat how neo-racism is crushing the life out of some of our best and brightest black youth in schools and colleges as well as in professional life. Our continuing concern will be to tell it like it is for black family members for a lifetime. While many white theologians are preoccupied with the unborn and the dying, the black theologian must be concerned about the abundant life for black folk between birth and death. Eternal life is a quality of life which the Christian begins in the new birth. It grows and continues into everlasting life. Black church theology provides a foundation for ministry to black men, women, and children *now.*

We are convinced by our study and the assessment of the empirical reality of black life that the black church has as a primary task the strengthening of black families. While the liberation of black men, women, and children, separately, must move forward, priority must be given to black families. Families are the "moral schools" for children. Our future as a people will be determined by how well we meet the needs of healthy black families. The relation of black families and churches is mutual. Failure of the black church to minister appropriately and urgently to black families will hasten its own death.

III. THE BLACK CHURCH AND FAMILY LIBERATION

We have attempted in these pages to show how the black church's theological self-understanding can lay a foundation for ministry to black families. American families are in trouble. Black families, as part of a racially oppressed community, are in deep trouble. Black families face internal problems, but the external situation often outweighs the inner tensions. Another way of stating the case is to argue that sinful social structures aggravate the inner tensions to unmanageable proportions.

We have studied the history and sociology of the black family and have allowed our doctrine of the church in the black tradition to emerge out of that context. The extended family has been employed as a way of imaging the black church. Since our goal has been to make these two primary black institutions mutually supportive, it has been proper to use the family image in reference to a black ecclesiology. The discussion has taken us into theological method, Biblical interpretation, and theological construction. Our task culminates in our focus upon the black church's ministry to black families. Since black families are the source of the black church's life and growth, the measure of its ministry to black families will determine the quality of its own mission. When the black church is viewed as a family, all persons, whether married, single, or divorced, will come to a sense of kinship in the church as the family of God. The church is the family under the Lordship of Jesus Christ, to whom all families in heaven and earth owe their substance and health. Let us hasten the day when the church will be a family and the family a domestic church. Then will God's Kingdom be nearer than we had believed.

Notes

CHAPTER I. AN INTRODUCTION

1. See W. E. B. Du Bois (ed.), *The Negro American Family* (Atlanta University, 1909; repr. MIT Press, 1970).

2. See E. Franklin Frazier, *The Negro Church in America* (Schocken Books, 1964), and his *The Negro Family in the United States* (University of Chicago Press, 1939; rev. and abr. ed., 1966). Frazier also wrote concerning black youth: cf. *Negro Youth at the Crossways* (1940; Schocken Books, 1967).

3. See Andrew Billingsley and Amy Tate Billingsley, *Black Families in White America* (Prentice-Hall, 1968); also Andrew Billingsley, *Black Families and the Struggle for Survival: Teaching Our Children to Walk Tall* (Friendship Press, 1974); (in collaboration with Jeanne M. Giovannoni), *Children of the Storm: Black Children and American Child Welfare* (Harcourt Brace Jovanovich, 1972); and an article on "The Black Church," in *The Black Scholar* (Dec. 1970), pp. 3–12. The author was in close association with Billingsley on black family and church studies while the latter served as vice-president for academic affairs at Howard University.

4. See Robert Staples (ed.), *The Black Family* (Wadsworth Publishing Co., 1971).

5. Carter G. Woodson, *The History of the Negro Church,* 3d ed. (Associated Publishers, 1972).

6. C. Eric Lincoln, *The Black Church Since Frazier* (bound with E. Franklin Frazier, *The Negro Church in America;* Schocken Books, 1973).

7. Hart M. Nelsen et al., *The Black Church in America* (Basic Books, 1971).

8. Even popular magazines are giving serious attention to this matter. See *Psychology Today,* May 1977, pp. 39ff.; *Newsweek,* May 15, 1978, pp. 63–90.

9. John Knox, *The Christian Answer,* p. 242. Quoted in Karl Ludwig Schmidt, "The Church," *Bible Key Words* (London: Adam & Charles Black, 1950), p. v.

10. J. Deotis Roberts, "Black Theology in the Making," *Review and Expositor,* Vol. LXX, No. 3 (Summer 1973), pp. 321–330.

11. Ibid., p. 330.

12. Allan A. Boesak, *Farewell to Innocence: A Socio-ethical Study on Black Theology and Black Power* (Orbis Books, 1977).

13. James Cone, *God of the Oppressed* (Seabury Press, 1978).

14. Levi A. Nwachuku, "Africa," *Black World,* Vol. XXV, No. 5 (March 1976), pp. 74–77.

15. Karl Barth, *Church Dogmatics,* I, 2; ed. by G. W. Bromiley and T. F. Torrance (Edinburgh: T. & T. Clark, 1956), p. 303.

16. Ibid., pp. 346–347.

17. Ibid., pp. 340–344.

18. Cone, *God of the Oppressed,* p. 112.

19. Ibid., p. 114.

20. Ibid.

21. Ibid.

22. Ibid., p. 135.

23. Ibid.

24. Ibid., p. 136.

25. Ibid.

26. Ibid., p. 137.

27. James H. Cone, "Black Theology and the Black Church," *Cross Currents,* Vol. XXVII, No. 2 (Summer 1977), pp. 147–156.

28. James H. Cone, "Report—Black and African Theologies: A Consultation," *Christianity and Crisis,* March 3, 1975. Essays from this consultation were published in *The Journal of Religious Thought,* Vol. XXXII, No. 2 (1975).

29. Charles Long, "Perspectives for a Study of Afro-American Religion in the United States," *History of Religions,* Vol. XI, No. 1 (August 1971), p. 54.

30. Ibid., p. 55.

31. Ibid., pp. 56–66.

32. Cone, "Report—Black and African Theologies," p. 51. Cf. C. H. Long, "Structural Similarities and Dissimilarities in Black and African Theologies," *The Journal of Religious Thought,* Vol. XXXII, No. 2 (Fall–Winter 1975), pp. 9–24.

33. J. Deotis Roberts, "Theology of Religions: The Black Religious Heritage," *Journal of the Interdenominational Theological Center,* Vol. I, No. 2 (Spring 1974), pp. 54–68.

34. Ibid., p. 67.

35. Amos N. Wilder, *Theopoetic: Theology and the Religious Imagination* (Fortress Press, 1976), p. 1.

36. Ibid.

37. Ibid.

38. Ibid., p. 25.

39. Ibid., pp. 25–26.

40. J. Deotis Roberts, *Faith and Reason* (Christopher Publishing House, 1962), pp. 37–38.

41. Paul Tillich, *Systematic Theology,* Vol. I (University of Chicago Press, 1951), p. 77; cf. Blaise Pascal, *Pensées,* 277.

42. J. Deotis Roberts, "Contextual Theology," *The Christian Century,* Jan. 28, 1976, pp. 64–68.

CHAPTER II. THE FAMILY IN THE BLACK EXPERIENCE

1. Walter F. Mondale, "The Family in Trouble," *Psychology Today,* May 1977, p. 39.

2. Ibid., pp. 41–47.

3. Ibid., p. 48.

4. *Newsweek,* May 15, 1978, pp. 77–78.

5. Ibid., pp. 89–90.

6. Lee Rainwater and William L. Yancey (eds.), *The Moynihan Report and the Politics of Controversy: A Trans-action Social Science and Public Policy Report; Including the Full Text of The Negro Family: The Case for National Action by Daniel Patrick Moynihan* (MIT Press, 1967), pp. 75–76.

7. Ibid., p 130.

8. Ibid.

9. Ibid., pp. 47–124. Cf. the 1978 figures in *Newsweek,* May 15, 1978, p. 77.

10. Ibid., p. 77.

11. Ibid.

12. Ibid., p. 78.

13. I cannot help being amused by such concerns as who will bathe and change the baby or what to do with two paychecks, at a time when the black family faces such gross hardships. See *The Los Angeles Times,* March 10, 1978, p. IV-4.

14. *The Los Angeles Times,* March 12, 1978, p. IV-13.

15. *The Los Angeles Times,* March 15, 1978, p. I-A-5.

16. Ibid., pp. 5–7.

17. Nathan Hare, "What Black Intellectuals Misunderstood About the Black Family," *Black World,* Vol. XXV, No. 5 (March 1976), pp. 4–14.

18. Ibid., p. 5.

19. Ibid., p. 6.

20. Ibid.

21. Ibid., p. 12.

22. Ibid.

23. Ibid.

24. Ibid.

25. At a conference held at Oklahoma City by the Oklahoma Association of Black Personnel in Higher Education (April 28–30, 1978), Nathan Hare and I gave lectures. There was an opportunity to explore the insights further. After Dr. Will Scott had made a statement about the need for blacks to have large families, even out of wedlock, a black pastor approached me to counter this suggestion. It was reinforcing to have Dr. Hare's presence and support. Ministers work directly with these families and not with figures and facts. Black theologians must evaluate studies, but they must not get too far from the church as a caring fellowship for persons. Much of Hare's work presently is focused upon personal counseling as a psychologist. This may account for his affinity with some concerns pastors have. In his Ph.D. thesis on psychology he has explored the important subject of black male-female relations.

26. See Alex Haley, *Roots* (Doubleday & Co., 1976; Dell Publishing Co., 1977).

27. Billingsley and Billingsley, *Black Families in White America,* pp. 39–40.

28. Ibid., p. 40.

29. Ibid., p. 48.

30. Nathan Glazer, "Introduction," in Stanley M. Elkins, *Slav-*

ery: A Problem in American Institutional and Intellectual Life (Grosset & Dunlap, 1963), p. ix.

31. Ibid., pp. xi–xii.

32. See the summary of Elkins' views stated by Thomas F. Pettigrew, *A Profile of the Negro American* (D. Van Nostrand Co., 1964), pp. 13–14.

33. Eugene D. Genovese, *Roll, Jordan, Roll: The World the Slaves Made* (Pantheon Books, 1974), pp. 4–6.

34. *Before the Mayflower: A History of the Negro in America* (Chicago: Johnson Publishing Co., 1964), pp. 30–31.

35. Billingsley and Billingsley, *Black Families in White America,* pp. 68–69.

36. E. Franklin Frazier, *The Negro Family in the United States,* rev. and abr. ed. (University of Chicago Press, 1966), pp. 73–78.

37. Ibid.

38. Ibid., p. 80.

39. Ibid., p. 82.

40. Ibid.

41. Ibid., p. 85.

42. Ibid., pp. 87–88.

43. *The Los Angeles Times,* May 22, 1978, p. 1. The headline reads: "50% Black Illegitimacy Rate Called Misleading." There are many reasons for the high illegitimacy rate. The scarcity of black males is a prime factor. Other factors are: the emotional satisfaction of motherhood for an oppressed girl or woman; and the permissive sexual climate. Thus, in addition to the historical picture, many present-day realities come into play. The fact is, however, that there is a history which we must take seriously if we are to find any solutions.

44. Frazier, *The Negro Family in the United States,* pp. 360–361.

45. Ibid., p. 362.

46. Ibid., p. 363. For an account of the place of the black mammy in slave society, see Jessie W. Parkhurst, "The Black Mammy in the Plantation Household," *Journal of Negro History,* Vol. XXIII (1938), pp. 349–369. (NOTE: *Journal of Negro History* will be referred to as JNH.) Cf. W. E. B. Du Bois (ed.), *The Negro American Family,* pp. 18–26.

CHAPTER III. THE CHURCH IN THE BLACK EXPERIENCE

1. Henry H. Mitchell, *Black Belief: Folk Beliefs of Blacks in America and West Africa* (Harper & Row, 1975), p. 9.

2. Ibid., p. 1.

3. I have traced this in folklore. See my "Folklore and Religion: The Black Experience," *The Journal of Religious Thought,* Vol. XXVII, No. 2 (Summer Supplement, 1970), pp. 5–15.

4. See Mitchell, *Black Belief,* p. 10.

5. John W. Blassingame, *The Slave Community* (Oxford University Press, 1972), pp. 17–18.

6. Mitchell, *Black Belief,* p. 10.

7. Ibid., p. 22.

8. Ibid.

9. Ibid., p. 23.

10. Gayraud S. Wilmore, *Black Religion and Black Radicalism* (Doubleday & Co., Anchor Books, 1973), p. 1.

11. Ibid., p. 4.

12. Ibid., p. 5.

13. Ibid., p. 37.

14. See Harry Hoetink, *Slavery and Race Relations in the Americas* (Harper & Row, 1973), p. 10.

15. Wilmore, *Black Religion and Black Radicalism,* p. 38.

16. Joseph R. Washington, Jr., *Black Religion: The Negro and Christianity in the United States* (Beacon Press, 1964), p. 33. Quoted by Wilmore, *Black Religion and Black Radicalism,* p. 38.

17. Genovese, *Roll, Jordan, Roll,* p. 210.

18. See Harry Sawyerr, *God: Ancestor or Creator?* (London: Longmans, Green & Co., 1970).

19. See Genovese, *Roll, Jordan, Roll,* pp. 211–213. Cf. J. O. Awolalu, "Sin and Its Removal in African Traditional Religion," *Journal of the American Academy of Religion,* Vol. XLIV, No. 2 (1976), pp. 275–287. Henry Mitchell is correct when he asserts that these religions have changed little in the past half millennium. There is no historical basis for Genovese's conclusions. See Mitchell, *Black Belief,* p. 24.

20. The reader who desires to pursue the religious beliefs of slaves should examine the following sources: Paul F. Boller, Jr., "Washington, the Quakers, and Slavery," JNH, Vol. XLVI (1961),

pp. 83–88; Roman J. Zorn, "The New England Anti-Slavery Society," JNH, Vol. XLII, No. 3 (July 1957), pp. 157–176; Jerome W. Jones, "The Established Virginia Church and the Conversion of Negroes and Indians, 1620–1760," JNH, Vol. XLVI (1961), pp. 12–23. A good, well-rounded study of African religion in the "diaspora" is Roger Bastide's *African Civilizations in the New World,* tr. by Peter Green (London: C. Hurst & Co.; New York: Harper & Row, 1971). See also J. H. Johnson, "The Mohammedan Slave Trade," JNH, Vol. XIII, No. 4 (Oct. 1928), pp. 478–491.

21. E. Franklin Frazier, *The Negro Church in America,* pp. 1–19.

22. Ibid., pp. 5–6.

23. Frazier takes exception to Du Bois on this matter, but we prefer Du Bois's reading. Ibid. See W. E. B. Du Bois, *Some Efforts of the American Negroes for Their Own Betterment* (Atlanta, 1898).

24. Miles Mark Fisher, *Negro Slave Songs in the United States* (Cornell University Press, 1953). This study was based upon Fisher's Ph.D. studies at Chicago Divinity School and was published by the American Historical Association. I am pleased to list Miles Mark Fisher as my mentor during my theological studies at Shaw University. As scholar, pastor, and preacher, he introduced his students to the rich spiritual tradition of blacks at a time when black consciousness was not in vogue.

25. Frazier, *The Negro Church in America,* pp. 1–19.

26. Preston Williams seems to accept in substance Frazier's view. See his "The Black Church: Origin, History, Present Dilemma," *McCormick Quarterly,* Vol. XXII (May 1969), p. 224. Williams draws a more militant conclusion, perhaps because of his involvement in the black struggle at that time.

27. James O. Buswell, *Slavery, Segregation and Scripture* (Wm. B. Eerdmans Publishing Co., 1964), p. 49.

28. Cf. Charles Colcock Jones, *A Catechism for Colored Persons* (Charleston, S.C.: Observer Office Press, 1834).

29. Fisher, *Negro Slave Songs in the United States,* pp. 79–81.

30. Ibid., pp. 81–82.

31. Ibid., p. 82.

32. Ibid., pp. 185–187.

33. Ibid., pp. 187–188. Cf. W. E. B. Du Bois, *The Souls of Black Folk* (Chicago, 1903), p. 190.

34. Fisher, *Negro Slave Songs in the United States,* p. 189.

35. Du Bois, *The Souls of Black Folk,* p. 261.

36. James H. Cone, *The Spirituals and the Blues* (Seabury Press, 1972), p. 15.

37. Ibid.

38. Benjamin E. Mays, *The Negro's God as Reflected in His Literature* (1938; Atheneum Press, 1968), pp. 21–28.

39. Howard Thurman, *The Negro Spiritual Speaks of Life and Death* (Harper & Brothers, 1947), p. 12. See his *Deep River* (1955; Kennikat Press, 1969). Recent talks with Thurman (May 18, 1978) confirm this outlook.

40. Harold A. Jackson, Jr., "The Negro Spiritual as Religious Expression and Historical Experience," *Journal,* The Blaisdell Institute, Claremont, Calif., Vol. XIV, No. 1 (Fall/Winter 1973–74), p. 42.

41. James H. Cone, *Black Theology and Black Power* (Seabury Press, 1969), pp. 94–95.

42. Ibid., pp. 96–97.

43. Ibid., p. 103.

44. Ibid., p. 91. Cone seems to accept Frazier's absolute destruction thesis. Since his main goal is political, it may not seem that important. But since it has to do with self-image and the identity crisis, it cannot be dismissed.

45. Wilmore, *Black Religion and Black Radicalism,* pp. 74–102.

46. Ibid., Chapter I.

47. Sergio Torres and Virginia Fabella (eds.), *The Emergent Gospel* (Orbis Books, 1976), p. 48.

48. Ibid., p. 88.

49. Ibid., p. 92.

50. See James H. Cone, *God of the Oppressed,* Chapters II and IV.

51. Cecil Wayne Cone, *The Identity Crisis in Black Theology* (Nashville: African Methodist Episcopal Church, 1975), p. 32.

52. Ibid., p. 64.

53. Ibid., pp. 71–72. For further reading on black religion during slavery, see: W. M. Brewer, "Henry Highland Garnet," JNH, Vol. XIII, No. 1 (1928), pp. 36–52; W. Edward Farrison, "A Theologian's Missouri Compromise," JNH, Vol. XLVIII (1963), pp. 33–43; James H. Smylie, "Uncle Tom's Cabin Revisited," *Interpretation,* Vol. XXVII, No. 1 (Jan. 1973), pp. 67–85; William C. Suttles,

Jr., "African Religious Survivals as Factors in American Slave Revolts," JNH, Vol. LVI, No. 2 (April 1971), pp. 97–104.

54. Stephen G. Taggart, *Mormonism's Negro Policy: Social and Historical Origins* (University of Utah Press, 1970), pp. 4–28.

55. Ibid., p. 16.

56. Ibid., p. 22.

57. Ibid., p. 28.

58. Ibid., pp. 33–36.

59. Ibid., pp. 37–38. Cf. Gordon H. Fraser, *What Does the Book of Mormon Teach?* (Moody Press, 1964), pp. 45–50. This is an example of the transference of color symbolism for theology.

60. W. R. Wilson, "The Religion of the American Negro Slave: His Attitude Toward Life and Death," JNH, Vol. VIII (1923), p. 41.

61. Ibid., p. 44.

62. Ibid., p. 46.

63. Ibid., p. 53.

64. Ibid., pp. 55–68.

65. Newbell N. Puckett, "Religious Folk Beliefs of Whites and Negroes," JNH, Vol. XVI (1931), p. 11.

66. Ibid., pp. 13–14.

67. Ibid., p. 18.

68. Ibid., p. 20.

69. Ibid., p. 23.

70. Ibid., p. 25.

71. Ibid., p. 22.

72. Ibid., p. 34. Cf. Robert M. Miller, "The Protestant Churches and Lynching, 1919–1939," JNH, Vol. XLII, No. 2 (1957), pp. 118–131; Douglas C. Strange, "Document: Bishop Daniel Alexander Payne's Protestation of American Slavery," JNH, Vol. LII, No. 4 (1967), pp. 59–64.

CHAPTER IV. BLACK CHURCH AND FAMILY: RECONSTRUCTION I TO RECONSTRUCTION II

1. Leon F. Litwack, *North of Slavery: The Negro in the Free States, 1790–1860* (University of Chicago Press, 1961), pp. 192–193. Cf. Monroe Fordham, *Major Themes in Northern Black Religious Thought, 1800–1860* (Exposition Press, 1975), pp. 73–83,

111–137. Studies that treat only the emotional tone of the black religious experience are important, but they do not give adequate attention to the "meaning" of black spirituality and often overlook the "protest" element altogether. See Raymond J. Jones, *A Comparative Study of Religious Cult Behavior Among Negroes; with Special Reference to Emotional Group Conditioning Factors,* Howard University Studies in the Social Sciences, Vol. II, No. 2 (Howard University Graduate School, 1939). Jones's study does, however, indicate real interest in the "material needs of the faithful" (p. 54).

2. A. Leon Higginbotham, Jr., "Virginia Led the Way in Legal Oppression," *The Washington Post,* May 21, 1978, Section 84. See his article "From Slavery to Bakke," *The Los Angeles Times* (July 2, 1978), pp. VI-1 to VI-3.

3. See Herbert G. Gutman, *The Black Family in Slavery and Freedom, 1750–1925* (Pantheon Books, 1976). Gutman argues that the black family was not split and demoralized by slavery. It is important that Alex Haley's *Roots* appeared about the same time. Gutman's book is well documented, but something went wrong with his sampling or his interpretation. There is no basis for optimism inherent in the slavery experience of blacks. It remains one of the cruelest human tragedies of the human race. Its scars are still upon all of black life. The blood and guilt of slavery belongs to the white descendants of slavemasters. Nothing short of collective repentance and corporate action will overcome the results of this "national sin." Black scholars, in all disciplines, must not allow nonblack scholars to smooth over this human tragedy in which we were victims and from which we still suffer as a people.

4. George Armstrong, *The Christian Doctrine of Slavery* (New York, 1857), pp. iii, 143, 9–64.

5. Ibid., p. 131. Cf. Archie C. Epps III, "The Christian Doctrine of Slavery: A Theological Analysis," JNH, Vol. XLVI (1961), pp. 243–249.

6. Other arguments by slavery theologians were based upon the curse of Ham or the practice of slavery among the Hebrews as well as arguments from the Pauline corpus in the New Testament. See Caroline L. Shanks, "The Biblical Anti-Slavery Argument," JNH Vol. XVI (1931), pp. 137–142.

7. Ibid., p. 145.

8. Ibid., pp. 153–154.

9. Ibid., p. 157.

10. "God Our Father, Christ Our Redeemer, Man Our Brother: A Theological Interpretation of the A.M.E. Church," *Journal of the Interdenominational Theological Center,* Vol. IV (Fall 1976), p. 26.

11. Ibid., pp. 27–28.

12. Ibid., p. 31.

13. Ibid., p. 32.

14. Ibid., p. 33.

15. Ibid. The following works will be useful as reflecting both the internal and external aspects of the formative period of the black churches before the Civil War: Charles H. Nichols, *Many Thousand Gone: The Ex-Slaves' Account of Their Bondage and Freedom* (Leiden: E. J. Brill, 1963); Milton C. Sernett, *Black Religion and American Evangelicalism: The Flowering of Negro Christianity 1787–1865,* American Theological Library Association Monograph Series, No. 1 (Scarecrow Press, 1975), pp. 59–81.

16. Nichols, *Many Thousand Gone,* p. 97.

17. Ibid., p. 96. Cf. the black self-understanding with slavery in the white mind. Elkins (*Slavery: A Problem in American Institutional and Intellectual Life,* 2d ed. (University of Chicago Press, 1968) has a syllogism to describe this outlook: "All slaves are black; slaves are degraded and contemptible; therefore all blacks are degraded and contemptible" (p. 61). He indicates how easily so-called "humane and decent Christians" accepted this view. Social taboos were a spinoff from this outlook. Hence we encounter laws against manumission, the horror of miscegenation, the depressed condition of free blacks, etc. We are told that slavery in the United States is not to be compared with slavery in the ancient world, which allowed for degrees of freedom and freedom itself. It is almost in contrast to Latin-American colonies of Spain and Portugal (pp. 62–80). It is Elkins' opinion that it was the capitalistic motivation behind the Southern agricultural economy which unchecked produced a "closed system" of slavery based upon skin color (p. 81). And yet by pushing the "Sambo" myth of black self-understanding, Elkins failed to realize the "radicalism" of black religion in slavery. See Timothy L. Smith, "Slavery and Theology: The Emergence of Black Christian Consciousness in the Nineteenth Century," *Church History,* Vol. XLI, No. 4 (Dec. 1972), p. 505. St. Clair Drake recalls how some blacks were persuaded of the notion that a return to Africa was their only hope for freedom and dignity. Many sincere white Christians pushed the return to Africa view for at least two

reasons: (1) some genuine concern for the relief of blacks from bondage; (2) a belief that slavery was a mixed blessing—it had introduced some Africans to Christianity and Western civilization which they could now share with Africans in heathendom. We are told that several black leaders accepted the philosophy and practice implied by this African colonization philosophy as their own and on this basis sought to participate in the "redemption of Africa." See St. Clair Drake, *The Redemption of Africa and Black Religion* (Institute of the Black World, 1970).

18. Ruby F. Johnston, *The Development of Negro Religion* (Philosophical Library, 1954).

19. Olin Moyd, "Redemption: A Theology from Black History" (unpublished Ph.D. dissertation, St. Mary's Seminary and University, Baltimore, 1976), pp. 88–90.

20. Ibid.

21. Ibid., pp. 106–107.

22. Ibid., p. 109.

23. Ibid., p. 110.

24. This was a period of wholesale lynchings in the South. The charge was often a real or contrived assault of a black male upon a white woman. White churches ignored, endorsed, or participated in this inhuman form of violence. See Robert Moats Miller, "Protestant Churches and Lynching, 1919–1939," JNH, Vol. XLII, No. 2 (1957), pp. 118–131.

25. Moyd, "Redemption," pp. 111–112.

26. Ibid., p. 118.

27. Ibid., p. 120.

28. Robert H. Brisbane, *The Black Vanguard: Origins of the Negro Social Revolution 1900–1960* (Judson Press, 1970), p. 166.

29. Joseph R. Washington, Jr., *Black Religion: The Negro and Christianity in the United States* (Beacon Press, 1964), p. 33.

30. Moyd, "Redemption," p. 123.

31. Ibid., p. 126.

32. See Kenneth Clark, "Race, Not Class, Is Still the Issue," *Current,* No. 203 (May-June 1978), pp. 19–22.

33. For further research on the impact of social, economic, and political history upon the black church (and family), see the following: Fordham, *Major Themes in Northern Black Religious Thought, 1800–1960,* pp. 13–17; Melvin D. Williams, *Community in a Black Pentecostal Church: An Anthropological Study* (University of Pitts-

burgh Press, 1974), pp. 3–16; Timothy L. Smith, "Slavery and Theology: The Emergence of Black Christian Consciousness in Nineteenth-Century America," *Church History,* Vol. XLI, No. 4 (Dec. 1972), pp. 497–512; Hart M. Nelsen and Anne K. Nelsen, *Black Church in the Sixties* (University Press of Kentucky, 1975), pp. 1–34, 98, 124–136; Robert M. Miller, "The Attitudes of American Protestantism Toward the Negro, 1919–1939," JNH, Vol. XLI (1956), p. 215; William H. Pipes, *Say Amen, Brother! Old-Time Negro Preaching* (William-Frederick Press, 1951), pp. i–5; Jon Butler, "Communities and Congregations: The Black Church in St. Paul, 1860–1900," JNH, Vol. LVI, No. 2 (April 1971), pp. 118–134; Benjamin E. Mays and Joseph W. Nicholson, *The Negro's Church* (1933; Russell & Russell, 1969), pp. 20–37. These are just some of the sources I found useful in moving through this part of the study.

34. Genovese, *Roll, Jordan, Roll,* p. 492.

35. Ibid., p. 491.

36. Frazier, *The Negro Family in the United States,* p. 134.

37. Ibid., pp. 134–135.

38. Jessie W. Parkhurst, "The Black Mammy in the Plantation Household," JNH, Vol. XXIII (1938), pp. 349–369.

39. Genovese, *Roll, Jordan, Roll,* p. 501.

40. Andrew Billingsley, "How Did the Black Family Remain Together?" *The Washington Star* (Sunday, Oct. 24, 1976), p. H-22.

41. Ibid. Cf. Holie I. West, "The Black Family: A New Perspective," *Washington Post* (Dec. 11, 1976), pp. E-1 to E-5; Richard Sennett, "The Black Family in Slavery and Freedom, 1750–1925," *The New York Times Book Review* (Oct. 17, 1978), pp. 3, 12.

42. Gutman, *The Black Family in Slavery and Freedom 1750–1925,* p. 3. Cf. John W. Blassingame, *The Slave Community: Plantation Life in the Antebellum South* (Oxford University Press, 1972), pp. 77–103.

43. Blassingame, *The Slave Community,* p. 103.

CHAPTER V. THE FAMILY OF GOD

1. James H. Cone, "Black Consciousness and the Black Church: A Historical-Theological Interpretation," unpublished paper, 1970. This essay appeared in *Frontier* (Spring 1970). The content of the essay is useful, but it is essentially Cone's reading of the history of

the black church. The need for a definitive historical-theological study of the black church remains. The task will no doubt require a team approach.

2. Roberts, *Liberation and Reconciliation: A Black Theology,* p. 60.

3. My use of "religion," singular, rather than "religions," plural, is deliberate. I am here more concerned with the unity than with the diversity of the African religious experience. See E. Bolaji Idowu, *African Traditional Religion: A Definition* (Orbis Books, 1973), pp. 106–107.

4. Blassingame, *The Slave Community,* p. 74.

5. Ibid., p. 75.

6. Ibid., p. 79. Cf. Albert J. Raboteau, *Slave Religion: The Invisible Institution in the Antebellum South* (Oxford University Press, 1978), Chapter V.

7. Kenneth L. Smith and Ira G. Zepp, Jr., *Search for the Beloved Community: The Thinking of Martin Luther King, Jr.* (Judson Press, 1974), p. 119.

8. Ibid., pp. 130–131.

9. Ibid., p. 119.

10. Gabriel M. Settiloane, "Confessing Christ Today," *Journal of Theology for Southern Africa,* No. 11 (July 1975), p. 31.

11. Ibid., p. 33.

12. Edward W. Fasholé-Luke, "Ancestor Veneration and the Communion of Saints," in Mark E. Glasswell and Edward W. Fasholé-Luke (eds.), *New Testament Christianity for Africa and the World* (London: SPCK, 1974), p. 214.

13. John A. T. Robinson, *The Body: A Study in Pauline Theology* (London: SCM Press, 1952; Philadelphia: Westminster Press, 1977), p. 9.

14. Ibid., pp. 58–61.

15. Howard Clark Kee, *Community of the New Age: Studies in Mark's Gospel* (Westminster Press, 1977), p. 138.

16. Ibid., p. 176.

CHAPTER VI. THE PEOPLE OF GOD

1. Hans Küng, *The Church* (Doubleday & Co., Image Books, 1976), p. 159.

2. Ibid., p. 160.

3. Ibid., p. 161.

4. John W. Blassingame (ed.), *Slave Testimony: Two Centuries of Letters, Speeches, Interviews, and Autobiographies* (Louisiana State University Press, 1977), pp. 457–459.

5. Ibid., p. 458.

6. Ibid., p. 461.

7. Ibid., p. 462.

8. Cf. Paul S. Minear, *Images of the Church in the New Testament* (Westminster Press, 1960), pp. 71–72.

9. Ibid., p. 78.

10. Ibid., p. 84.

11. William A. Jones, *The Black Church Looks at the Bicentennial* (Elgin, Ill.: Progressive National Baptist Publishing House, 1976), p. 123.

12. Ibid.

13. "Same God" in Langston Hughes and Arna Bontemps (eds.), *The Book of Negro Folklore* (Dodd, Mead & Co., 1958), p. 257.

14. Ibid., p. 305.

15. Ibid., p. 228.

16. Ibid., p. 76.

17. See Jer. 8:22; cf. Ps. 137:1–4.

18. Minear, *Images of the Church in the New Testament,* p. 167.

19. Ibid.

20. Johannes Pedersen, *Israel: Its Life and Culture,* Vols. I–II (London: Oxford University Press, 1926), p. 14.

21. Idowu, *African Traditional Religion,* pp. 179–188.

22. Minear, *Images of the Church in the New Testament,* p. 167.

23. Ibid., pp. 168–170.

24. Olli Alho, *The Religion of the Slaves: A Study of the Religious Tradition and Behaviour of Plantation Slaves in the United States 1830–1865* (Helsinki: Suomalainen Tiedeakatemia/Academia Scientiarum Fennica, 1976), p. 234.

25. Ibid., p. 233.

26. Olin P. Moyd, *Redemption in Black Theology* (Judson Press, 1979), pp. 23–24.

CHAPTER VII. THE BLACK CHURCH'S MINISTRY—
PRIESTLY AND PROPHETIC

1. C. Eric Lincoln, "The Black Family, the Black Church and the Transformation of Values," *Religion in Life,* Vol. XLVII, No. 4 (Winter 1978), p. 488.

2. Ibid., pp. 488–489.

3. Howard Thurman, *The Negro Spiritual Speaks of Life and Death* (Harper & Brothers, 1947).

4. Mays, *The Negro's God as Reflected in His Literature* (Atheneum Press, 1968).

5. Joseph A. Johnson, Jr., *The Soul of the Black Preacher* (Pilgrim Press, 1971).

6. W. E. B. Du Bois, *The Souls of Black Folk* (1903; Fawcett, 1977). Cf. Chapter 14 in his *The Gift of Black Folk* (1924; Washington Square Press, 1970).

7. Cecil W. Cone, *The Identity Crisis in Black Theology* (Nashville: African Methodist Episcopal Church, 1975).

8. Henry J. Young, *Major Black Religious Leaders 1755–1940* (Abingdon Press, 1977).

9. C. Eric Lincoln, "Black Church," *Christianity and Crisis,* Vol. XXX, No. 18 (Nov. 16, 1970), p. 226.

10. See Joseph H. Jackson, *Nairobi: A Joke, a Junket, or a Journey?* (Townsend Press, 1976), p. 69. His criticisms are aimed primarily at James Cone's program, but in fact he rejects all black theology as we now know it.

11. Joseph A. Johnson, Jr., *Proclamation Theology* (Shreveport, La.: Fourth Episcopal District C.M.E. Press, 1977), p. 126.

12. Joseph R. Washington, Jr., "How Black Is Black Religion?" in James J. Gardiner and J. Deotis Roberts (eds.), *Quest for a Black Theology* (Pilgrim Press, 1971), p. 28.

13. See Harold A. Carter, *The Prayer Tradition of Black People* (Judson Press, 1976).

14. Edward P. Wimberly, "The Suffering God," in Henry J. Young (ed.), *Preaching on Suffering and a God of Love* (Fortress Press, 1978), pp. 61–62.

15. Henry H. Mitchell, "Towards a Black Evangelism," *Journal of Religious Thought,* Vol. XXXV, No. 1 (1978), p. 65.

16. For those interested in pastoral care, Edward Wimberly's

book is a necessary manual for ministry in the black church: *Pastoral Care in the Black Church* (Abingdon Press, 1979).

17. Michele Wallace, *Black Macho and the Myth of the Superwoman* (Dial Press, 1979). See especially Chapter 3 for her views on black women and the "myth of the superwoman."

18. Ibid., p. 164.

19. Ibid., p. 165.

20. Ibid., p. 167.

21. Ibid., pp. 167–168.

22. E. Franklin Frazier, *The Negro Family in the United States* (1939), rev. and abr. ed. (University of Chicago Press, 1966), pp. 93–94.

23. Ibid., p. 95.

24. As reported by Bill Drummond in *The Los Angeles Times,* May 22, 1978, p. 1.

25. Michele Wallace, *Black Macho and the Myth of the Superwoman,* p. 172.

26. Inez Smith Reid, *"Together" Black Women* (Emerson Hall Publishers, 1972), Chapter II. Cf. Robert G. Weisbord, *Genocide? Birth Control and the Black American* (Greenwood Press, 1975).

27. Ibid., pp. 120–121.

28. Edward V. Stein (ed.), *Fathering, Fact or Fable?* (Abingdon Press, 1977), p. 11. Cf. William Raspberry, "Their Father Made the Difference," *The Washington Post,* June 15, 1979, p. A-17. According to Raspberry, Lee Junious, a black father, uneducated, unemployed, divorced, manages to inspire four kids to excel in school.

29. Ibid., p. 12.

30. Nathan Hare, "The Frustrated Masculinity of the Negro Male," in Robert Staples (ed.), *The Black Family: Essays and Studies* (Wadsworth Publishing Co., 1971), pp. 131–134.

31. Ibid., p. 133.

32. Alvin F. Poussaint, "Sex and the Black Male," *Ebony,* Aug. 1972, p. 115. This entire article (pp. 114–120) is worth reading. We cannot make further reference to it here. Cf. Gwendolyn Cooke, "Socialization of the Black Male," in Lawrence E. Gary (ed.), *Social Research and the Black Community* (Washington, D.C.: Institute for Urban Affairs and Research, 1974), pp. 76–87.

33. Robert Staples, "The Myth of Black Macho: A Response to

Angry Black Feminists," *Black Scholar,* March/April 1979, p. 28. *13*
Brenda Daniels-Eichelberger, "Myths About Feminism," *Essence,*
Nov. 1978, pp. 74ff. Cf. Marguerete Ross Barnett, "Black Male-
Female Relationship," *Washington Star,* July 1, 1979, a review of
Michele Wallace, *Black Macho and the Myth of the Superwoman.*
See also Marcia Ann Gillespie, "Macho, Myths and Michele Wal-
lace," *Essence,* Aug. 1979, pp. 76–102. Police killings account for
a large number of deaths of black males. Most of these killings are
of youths under twenty-five. See *Engage/Social Action,* Forum 46
(Nov.-Dec. 1978), especially the report by Lennox S. Hinds, Direc-
tor, National Conference of Black Lawyers (p. 16).

34. Ibid., p. 29.

35. Ibid.

36. Ibid., p. 31.

37. "Number of Children in Divorces Triples" in *Los Angeles
Times,* July 2, 1979, p. I-19.

38. James P. Comer and Alvin F. Poussaint, *Black Child Care*
(Simon & Schuster, 1975), p. 11.

39. Ibid.

40. Ibid., p. 12.

41. Cf. Howard J. Clinebell and Charlotte Clinebell, *Crisis and
Growth: Helping Your Troubled Child* (Fortress Press, 1971). Some
sources on black children and youth worth reading are: George B.
Thomas, *Young Black Adults: Liberation and Family Attitudes*
(Friendship Press, 1974); Andrew Billingsley and Jeanne M. Gi-
ovannoni, *Children of the Storm: Black Children and American
Child Welfare* (Harcourt Brace Jovanovich, 1972); Phyllis Harri-
son-Ross and Barbara Wyden, *The Black Child: A Parent's Guide*
(Peter H. Wyden, 1974); and E. Franklin Frazier, *Negro Youth at
the Crossways* (1940; Schocken Books, 1967).